How to Self-Publish When You Aren't Tech Savvy

A Clear-Cut Guide about How (and Why) to Publish a Book

Casey Callanan, MBA

DEDICATION

To all my friends and family that have supported my
writing over the years. Thank you.

CONTENTS

ACKNOWLEDGMENTS

I'm so thankful I have a core group of friends and family that have always been there for me. Self-publishing any of my books would have been impossible without your support.

CHAPTER 1
Time to Set Expectations

If you are serious about writing, and you really want to do it, there is nothing stopping you from self-publishing your first book.

There are no gatekeepers in this industry to stop you anymore.

Writing a book is a popular bucket list item for a worthy reason. To some folks, there may not be a more important way to leave your legacy. It's not uncommon for people to want to write a book towards the retirement years of their life. Writing a book about everything you've learned could be the perfect way to highlight a remarkable accomplishment or career in business, the arts, etc.

If you write a book that people want to read, it could be around for millennia. That's just a reality. A book can be an incredibly strong legacy. However, there is no reason to wait until retirement to write. You can write a book at any stage of life.

Right now, it has never been easier to physically publish a book.

Amazon's Kindle Direct Publishing (KDP) is the best option available to publish your own book. While this software/service is technology-based, you definitely do not have to be tech-savvy to navigate it.

Getting a manuscript up on this platform is straightforward. If you can't figure it out, there are plenty of workarounds to employ to get the job done. Online book publishers (such as KDP) will make more money with the more users that are able to understand and become proficient with their platforms. This means they have an economic incentive to make it as easy as possible for you to learn their software.

To use Amazon's service as an example, once your manuscript is approved by KDP, your book will be available for purchase on their website. This will allow your book to serve as a legacy for future generations to learn about you and your story. All of this has never been easier to do.

However, now is the time for me to be brutally honest. Since, at least in theory, anyone can publish a book right now, this could lead to a very "watered down" standard for published books. We may be approaching a day where it is increasingly less prestigious to have a book published.

Naysayers may look at this as a net negative overall. Someone who is not mentally strong enough to deal with this new reality may be a bit disappointed.

With the emergence of these new publishing technologies comes with it more opportunities and personal responsibilities. Some people will always take advantage of a system and try to publish an inferior book simply for money (or for some other scam).

I can live with that because I am now afforded a route to publish my own novels in a way that was impossible in the 1990s. Let's not let a few bad apples ruin the big picture of how great this new reality is for us.

I am very optimistic about this time in publishing, as long as we understand there are some personal responsibilities for each of us. Despite the accessibility of self-publishing, I truly encourage you to take the thorough steps in the manuscript production process and not cut any corners.

Let's try to live up to those historical standards of prestige in publishing a book.

You now have that responsibility, but let's look on the bright side. Think of how great it is that you don't have to go through a traditional publisher, and pray they call you back after a meeting where you pitched your manuscript.

All of the power rests in your hands now. We've democratized publishing through technology! (Rest assured, you can physically publish a book, even if you have no interest in technology.)

Carefully abide by the steps I outline in this book and refuse to cut corners. Together we can prove that an independent author can publish a book that can always match (or surpass) the quality of one from a traditional publisher.

First things first, I would like you to think deeply about why you want to write this book. I urge you to write it down. Have it be your personal mission statement. It can be your "north star" and keep you on track when adversity hits.

You need to be honest with yourself about the skills you bring to the table and the skills that you lack. Self-awareness is so important to all of this.

You have to be honest with yourself about your limitations as a writer. Please understand that writing a book can be difficult because of writing's subjective nature. Writing is unlike working on a home improvement project, cooking, or planting a garden. It's not a project that has a set beginning and a tangible end.

It's not a task that is necessarily "done" after a certain amount of hours you have put forth. You may have realized after four straight hours of writing that you were way off the whole time! What you wrote just doesn't make sense and won't work! This is especially true when writing fiction and developing story arcs.

Be patient, resilient, and relentless. Quality writing is difficult to pinpoint. It's very abstract. You could be writing all day, but it could be complete garbage. (Trust me, I have definitely been guilty of this!)

It's important to understand that unlike cooking a meal where you know something will be started at a certain point and finished at another point, writing is not linear. Just because you write all day doesn't mean that it is good, or even that it's understandable.

The harsh reality is that just because you put the time into writing doesn't mean it's anything worthy of being published. That's the truth of writing that I need to convey in this first chapter before you get started.

Do you see why having a thick skin and being very persistent is extremely important in writing?

Unless you allow an editor to objectively review your manuscript, and allow them to give you honest and constructive feedback, you'll never really know if what you've been doing is even worth a hoot. Feelings may get hurt, but this is all part of the book-producing mission.

Even if you fail, making an effort towards your writing is always, at the very least, going to give you something tangible to learn from. Practice is always a good thing in these endeavors. At the very least, you have gained experience.

Before you start writing, establish why you want to write this book.

Do you want to provide others the chance to learn about you, or your experiences, in perpetuity? That's noble. It's also probably one of the most important reasons for writing a book. And thus, you need to take it very seriously when you embark on this endeavor.

You need to strike a balance between being decisive and carefully taking your time to make sure you say things precisely. You really want future generations to understand you. If you're writing nonfiction or a historical account of something, it's probably not in your best interest to leave any gray area.

If it's nonfiction, why would you want to leave anything open to interpretation?

Writing a book for the sole purpose of making money is a questionable choice. I don't recommend it if it's your only source of income, and you're relying on it to pay the bills (unless you are an established author). You'll need to make sure you have other sources of income coming in as book sales can be as fickle as an afternoon on the golf course.

If you're a business owner, or someone looking to start a business, writing a book can establish your expertise on certain subjects, but it probably won't be enough on its own to build your enterprise.

That said, it's definitely possible to write a book as a way to make some passive income and earn a royalty check. While it might make sense if you are a known writer, or journalist, who is out of work to expect a nice check after your well-constructed book is published, it's probably not realistic for most folks. Don't make it hard on yourself and expect it to replace your 9-to-5 gig.

If you're self-publishing a book, you can't put that much pressure on yourself and expect this entire endeavor to replace your salary if you have a family and other people depending on you to "win the bread."

Setting expectations about why you are writing the book in the first place is key. Think deeply about why you want to do it.

If it's a fiction story that you've been wanting to tell, then you have to get it out in front of other people and make sure that you're taking it to writing groups where people are poking holes in it. Editors and proofreaders are always our friends.

Do you understand the essence of a story arc? Make sure you've done your due diligence here. There are elements to structuring a fiction narrative and coherent plot that, at the very least, you should be familiar with when structuring your story.

Expecting your book to be a vehicle for increasing your overall happiness by challenging yourself is probably a safe place to start.

Perhaps someday down the line, having your book on Amazon could boost your income, but don't forget there are costs associated with self-publishing a book. It is free to utilize Amazon's self-publishing platform, KDP, but hiring freelancers to edit your copy, and a designer to create your book's cover costs money.

Roughly speaking, a few hundred dollars should be what you can expect to budget for this entire project. Relative to the expenses of what it used to cost writers to publish a book and store the extra inventory, these costs are very modest. Let's always look on the bright side.

Adversity will find you when writing a book, so practice building up that thick skin, and make resiliency your top character trait.

Setting financial expectations for when you write this book means being mentally prepared to lose money on this book. Create a budget upfront and stick with it. Depending on your book's length, you may pay anywhere from $50 to $500 on a copy-editor, and $50 to $100 to have your book cover created.

These estimates should give you a rough estimate of the amount of money involved.

You have to look within and identify your limitations as a writer after your financial expectations and budget are solidified.

Like I said at the very beginning of this chapter, it's ultimately up to us to ensure the standards of having a published book on the open market do not get diminished.

In this society, it is still very much viewed as a prestigious thing to write and publish a book; let's keep that legacy and reputation of a published book strong. It's on our shoulders. One of the first things you have to do before you set out to write a book, or publish a manuscript, is to be completely honest with yourself as to what your writing chops are. How good of a writer are you?

Being honest with what our limitations and weaknesses are as a writer is one of the most difficult things we have to do. Just because you're not the greatest writer in the world, does not mean you can't self-publish a book—help is always available! It's the ideas that are the most valuable thing here. The actual prose can always be honed and improved upon with the aid of editors and co-authors.

You might not be a good writer at all, but that does not mean you can't publish a book. There are other options available. There are so many memoirs out there "written" by people who have zero writing ability.

This is because they found co-authors and ghostwriters to take their ideas and turn them into quality prose. Ideas, concepts, and stories are at the foundation of a great book, and that has to come from you, but help is available to assist with the actual prose.

It's going to cost you a little bit more money to bring these people on unless you somehow know folks who will do it for free, so adjust your budget accordingly.

These people can help you formulate the way you want to say the great ideas and stories that are rattling around inside your head.

Be honest with yourself about your writing chops and identify where you need help. You might have to reach out to people on different websites, such as Fiverr.com, Upwork.com, Craigslist, etc. The overhead costs to produce this book will grow because of hiring specialists—factor all of that into your budget.

There is reason to believe that one day you can recoup some of these costs, and maybe even make a profit on the book, but keep your costs down unless you have an airtight marketing strategy to sell it.

If these are your stories and ideas, and you're just not that great of an actual writer, it's okay. The real talent that is going to catch people's attention are the plotlines and concepts, not necessarily how much you razzle-dazzle people with prose.

Many great writers out there can really formulate opinions flawlessly with the written word. It's still a coveted skill to be a good writer, but as we've seen with the proliferation of blogs and the written word on the internet, there are many writers available for hire.

There will never be a lack of capable writers, but there will certainly always be a lack of compelling stories, concepts, and ideas that need to be told. With that in mind, if you have these ideas you want to get out there, but you lack the writing chops, there are people out there that can help you immensely.

It's possible your first book is going to end up being your most notable book, so it's important to make a big splash with it. That first book is like making your first impression. To make a splash with this first impression, you'll want to build a sustainable writing habit to publish the best possible book.

Building a writing habit is so important.

The number one thing to do is make sure you're building a writing habit once your self-publishing project gets rolling. Getting into a habit of writing is crucial for people who have a normal job and grapple with the demanding responsibilities life always throws our way.

You need to find a certain amount of time on a consistent basis that you will devote to writing. You can also spend that designated time doing something that's helping get you closer to your self-publishing goals.

I throw that second part in there because we are not robots. Some days we have more ability (or inspiration) to write more than other days. It's not linear, so when we aren't feeling much like Hemingway on a certain day, those are the times to do administrative tasks that move us towards our self-publishing goals.

Administrative tasks include researching how to use Fiverr.com to hire a book cover designer, watching YouTube videos about how to use KDP, etc.

All these tasks bring us closer to the ultimate goal of self-publishing a book. They can be done during that designated "writing time" we have established.

I like to think of the *floss your teeth metaphor* when I describe the importance of building a writing habit. Here's how I can best explain that metaphor:

When you're trying to build a habit of flossing your teeth, it's just important to create that muscle memory. I've heard experts say that in order to get people into the habit of flossing their teeth, they recommend that at first you just floss one tooth per night.

If you just get in the habit of flossing that one tooth per night, eventually you're going to build in that muscle memory where you get out the floss, open it up, and you floss that tooth. The next thing you know, you start flossing two teeth per night, then three teeth. The idea is that at some point down the line you'll be flossing your entire mouth because you built in the muscle memory.

It's the same concept I want you to take towards writing.

Even if you just write one sentence per day in the beginning, you will be building that habit. When you write that one sentence out on paper on a regular basis at the properly designated time, you are building the muscle memory and that habit of sitting down at the computer, opening up the word processor, etc.

Try it. Write one sentence at your designated "writing time" each day (or every other day) and then go back to whatever other tasks you are doing. As long as you are consistent, it will work. Consistency is the keyword.

It's challenging for me to look at a blank piece of paper and start writing. (Mind you, this is coming from an author who has written all of his life).

Writer's block seems to hit me harder when I sit in front of a blank screen as I set out to write, but there's a way to avoid it.

You can actually dictate some of your books on a microphone and then have it transcribed! This little trick works wonders for me. After I have my spoken words transcribed, I then go back and do a major editing job with the transcription as I rewrite all of the content. I do this during my designated "writing time."

All of this rewriting of a transcript is definitely a lot of work, but I found it to be easier than staring at a blank piece of paper every night when I sit down to write. Either way, building that consistent writing habit and identifying which way to write works best for you is the most important thing to actually getting a book written and published.

After you've set your expectations, and you've understood what your writing abilities are, the next step is building that writing habit. There's nothing I love to do more than write. I've known since I was a teenager that writing was essentially my life's calling.

I find myself in my most confident state of mind when I am writing. It's comforting and centers me. I feel weird if time has gone by and I haven't been writing. All does not feel well in my world unless I am writing on a regular basis. However, even though I am so passionate about writing, and have these aspects of it built deep within my DNA, I struggle with finding time to write consistently.

(I don't say this to discourage you, I just want to be a straight shooter with you at all times.)

If you take it seriously, you will be able to build a sustainable writing habit. We've all done much harder things!

Having that regular writing time is the only way, in my opinion, to get a quality manuscript written. This is just my opinion, but as a writer, I know that I can't just binge write.

Binge writing has never worked for me.

I can't just sit down, isolate myself for 8 hours, five days in a row, and bang out a script like that. I've tried it, trust me.

I've tried to sit there and work for hours and hours and days on end, just to write a book, but it doesn't work for me that way. I'll go stir crazy, drink too much coffee, and spin my wheels.

I'm pretty sure it probably won't work for you too. Binge writing isn't for most folks, but there are always exceptions to the rule.

The quality just seems to dip (at least for me) when I engage in binge writing. I become physically tired, mentally drained, and the written word just does not flow as good during a "binge" for me.

Be persistent. The consistent dedication to your craft is what will separate you from the pack.

Writing a book, much like the construction of Rome, is not something you can do in one day. It's something that you have to work hard at building overtime to do properly. Continuously move that book forward in small chunks. Be unrelenting in your consistency.

No matter what your writing ability may be, and regardless of your expectations for this book, persistence is the key to it all.

This is the most accessible time in the history of publishing. Let that be your motivation. Be aware that this *could* change. It's not a guarantee that this infrastructure that is currently in place to self-publish a book so affordably on KDP will always be this way. Time may be of the essence here, folks. Nothing is guaranteed.

Since it has never been easier to self-publish, I also think that leaves us with a lot of responsibility. We cannot, as serious writers or readers, allow the quality of a self-published book to dip on our watch!

Let's uphold the standards and reputation that a published book so rightfully deserves. As we'll discuss later, the approval process is very fair for getting a book self-published on KDP, but remember that *could* change.

If you're not willing to go through all these steps, then maybe it's best to consider some alternative storytelling options, such as podcasting or blogging. On the other side, no matter what your individual situation may be, as long as you have an unbreakable desire to self-publish a book, you can do it.

I firmly believe a published book will serve you well and be worth all of the effort. It could even be your most remembered legacy on this planet.

CHAPTER 2

The Art of the Written Word

We live in a very interesting media age. The accessibility and democratization of self-publishing are unprecedented. The tough part of this media environment is that it's super easy to get distracted. Distraction is the writer's kryptonite.

This same media landscape that's granted us a very manageable path to self-publishing a book has also made it easier than ever for us to get distracted and forget about writing.

Many people these days tend to complete a majority of their business and career responsibilities on their smartphones. This might include anything as simple as responding to emails and composing social media posts.

Opening up your phone creates a host of temptations and places to get distracted. And again, distraction is the kryptonite to an accomplished writer, in my view.

Even when you get on your laptop or desktop computer, it is easy to get distracted. One Facebook or Twitter notification might throw you off your writing tasks for an hour.

With these lurking distractions, people have returned to writing novels with simple pen and paper.

Some may even use a typewriter. These are hardly drastic measures if you realize how derailing distractions can be for a writer.

People have gone as far as to make sure their internet is disconnected before they write. Build a habit where you are writing regularly and employ willpower to avoid distractions.

Having willpower is the only sustainable way, in my opinion, to really get writing done and avoid the distractions. Writing without having to rely on different tricks like cutting off your own internet is the habit you should be looking to build.

I don't think you have to go to such an extreme, but sometimes there are some little strategies I'll employ to help me avoid potential distractions. For example, if I'm writing on a train and I know they have free WiFi, I'll avoid the temptation by going without it for the duration of the ride.

Be aware of how you write best. What writing environment best suits your style? Do you like it so quiet that you can hear a pin drop, or do you like the television on in the background as white noise when you write?

Whatever helps you focus and get you into your "writing zone" is key. Identify the setting that works best for you and fight to have that be a staple of your routine. In an offshoot of my apartment, there is an office where I go to shut the door, focus, and write. It's what works for me.

I know that over the years in different forms of media (movies, tv shows, etc.), there has been a certain air of romance associated with writing and the lifestyle of a writer. You know the archetype of a writer locked away in their beachside estate, writing all day a la John Steinbeck in Monterey, California, or Ernest Hemingway in Key West, Florida.

These are the romantic notions that tend to go along with the novelist and writer. Maybe it's the idea of David McCullough locked away in his coastal Massachusetts cottage as the beautiful summer evening sun sets on the Atlantic. There's a lot of different notions and romanticisms that people have about the novelist and writing.

In reality, writing is very frustrating. Writing can be very difficult. It is full of hard work and requires sacrifice. It is hardly glamorous, but it can be fun.

That's the fickle reality of writing. It's hard work, but it pays off. It's like being in the gym. It might not be something you can enjoy in the exact moment that you are doing it, but you will be happy you did it when it's done. Writing is something you have to readjust your expectations about.

For example, McCullough and his team of researchers spend months on end going to different libraries and historical sites doing the legwork for his novels. Given this immense preparation, I'd assume the actual writing is the icing on the cake. The blood, sweat, and tears (so to speak) comes within the research stages of the project.

Not everyone's novels will need to be researched to that end, but I definitely want to make you aware of the length that some of us will need to go to in order to make a self-published book a successful reality.

Now, if you're going to write a historical novel, then prepare to get your "research hat" on. This book doesn't delve deeply into the research aspect of writing a book. This is not a book about how to conduct research. However, the research needed for your book can take an incredible amount of effort and be a full-time job in and of itself. What I'm encouraging you to do here is understand the amount of time you might need to put forth to do your best work.

Some of the greatest writers ever tend to be associated with romantic notions. We may think about them as locked away in a mountain top cabin with breathtaking views. I imagine Hunter S. Thompson hammering away on a typewriter in Woody Creek, Colorado.

I picture him in this manic state of flow while writing these beautiful pieces of prose flowing out of his fingertips.

While there are people that enter a flow-like psychological state of mind when they write, these are the exceptions rather than the rule.

Writers like Charles Dickens, Thompson, and Steinbeck are far from the standard. Yet, because they are overwhelmingly portrayed in the media, it can be harder to lose sight of how rare this style of writing is.

Movies and television shows don't tend to depict the far more practical and exceedingly less glamourous writing style of normal people. This could entail coming home from a day of teaching 8th graders, having dinner on the table for your family, and then quietly typing out a few paragraphs to keep your manuscript on track before bed.

In reality, writing entails deep sacrifices. Many other things you could be doing are far more enjoyable.

All of us will need to make sacrifices to write our best possible book. There is an opportunity cost involved in writing a book. I'm not saying that instead of taking the grandkids out for ice cream, you should be holed up in your office writing, but maybe instead of investing 12-hours in watching a new six-part series on Netflix, you spend the time writing. You can just read the Wikipedia page (cliff notes version) about the documentary instead, and then spend the balance of that time you've saved writing!

I used to think of Hemingway and associate him with a hedonistic lifestyle. I picture him going fishing in the morning, writing for a few hours at night, then waking up the next morning and doing it all again. Perhaps there could not be a more relaxed and beautiful lifestyle. However, this was probably far from reality. If Hemmingway ever did reach that lifestyle, it probably took decades and decades of sacrifice to get there.

After publishing three books and writing my butt off for the last couple of years, I respect how challenging it is to write. To write is to work.

I really enjoy journaling, but that is different from writing a novel because I know that it won't be published. With that freedom in mind, I allow myself to express my feelings as an open stream of consciousness.

While it can be relaxing to do things like keep a journal about your life and feelings, this is different than writing for an audience. (On a side note, I encourage everyone to keep a journal, because it is great practice and does tend to make you a better overall writer.)

When you've decided that you're writing a book, it's time to get serious about your writing process. There becomes a tangible end goal at this point, and it might not be a linear process.

I say this because maybe someone who's reviewing your manuscript notices that something is blatantly wrong with what you've been writing. It's not unheard of to have to start from scratch after someone has reviewed your work. Be prepared to rip everything down and start again.

Expect the worst, hope for the best.

That's why I want to warn you that writing can be full of frustration, and the characteristics that prevail in writing include having resilience, a thick skin, and tunnel vision.

Is it a coincidence that some of the great writers of our day, such as Hunter S. Thompson and the like, were passionate about boxing? Well, I do not think it's a coincidence, because the same characteristics that make a great prizefighter make for a great writer too.

For most of us Non-Hemmingway folk, we cannot expect to be locked away in a cabin writing until the sun sets. That is probably impractical, given your daily responsibilities. I also find it crucially important to break up my writing cycles into bite-sized and manageable efforts.

There will be days when your brain feels fresher than other days. There will be days where you feel invincible and strong. You should really take advantage of those days and push the limits of how much you can write when you're feeling strong. Life is not linear nor predictable as we have good and bad days as wishy-washy as the wind.

If you expand your definition of "writing," you will find yourself being more productive with administrative tasks that are necessary to publish a book on the days when you're not feeling like a great novelist.

Every little step in the right direction towards getting your book published counts. This is why it's important to avoid these unsustainable binge writing days.

Writing on a binge isn't the way to build a proper writing habit.

Try to get into a regular habit of establishing time that you work towards writing (or doing anything that helps you get your book published).

You'll be amazed by how much that's going to help you inch closer to your self-publishing goal with consistency.

I've definitely fallen victim to procrastinating when I should be writing. Distractions can run amok in my life (many of which I could be controlling), and I've wasted precious writing time that I'll never get back.

Distractions and procrastinations invade our lives in many clever forms. You might notice that your refrigerator, all of a sudden, seems to get really clean when you know you should have been writing. Maybe there's not a speck of dust in your office anymore a few moments after you realize you should have been writing for the past hour.

All of a sudden, the vacuuming in your apartment gets done, and your spouse arrives home, commenting on how pristine it's gotten. While these are good things, they are also signs of procrastination.

If you find yourself dusting a window when you should be writing, you really need to catch yourself.

It's important to be conscious in those moments of what we're actually doing, and that's avoiding what's really hard: writing. While we all know writing is hard, you may be surprised to find the hardest part is actually getting started. Once you start writing, it's typically all good from there.

(That's similar to going to the gym for me. The toughest part is the actual physical moving of my feet to get to the darn place. Once I'm there, and I've avoided every excuse in the book not to be there, it's all good.)

While you may be realizing the benefits of an impeccably clean office lately, the reality is you've been avoiding the more difficult task at hand, which is writing.

Don't get me wrong, that office could still be clean, you just have to make sure you're prioritizing your time and tasks properly.

Given the fact that writing can be so difficult, think about if any previous writing that you've done makes sense to combine into an anthology with a central theme. Maybe it's a journal you kept during a memorable summer when you went backpacking in Europe, or a blog that you used to write for a website you forgot about.

Is there a central theme to some writing you've done in the past? It could be a gateway to a foundation for publishing your first book. The journal entries would give you the base, and then you could expand upon why this experience changed you and tell stories about what you learned.

It will definitely take a ton of editing and time to take a series of journal entries or blogs and turn them into a book. However, it also may be easier than starting from scratch.

For example, when I was in college at West Virginia University, I consistently wrote a blog for SportingNews.com about the WVU football and basketball program. That time in West Virginia athletics ended up being historical as the football team was fighting for a shot at winning the National Championship each year.

The basketball team was incredible as well. They went to the NCAA Final Four and won the National Invitational Tournament (NIT) around the same span of time I was writing this sports blog.

What I could have done (and wish I had done) was saved all of those blogs and created a book aimed at the audience of West Virginia sports fans. This is a passionate crew that loves to consume media about their beloved Mountaineers. I believe I would have written a gem while reflecting on this historical period of West Virginia sports, using the blogs as my starting point.

It could have been my first book! Unfortunately, the idea to do this didn't come to me until years after I had graduated. By the time I thought about doing it, SportingNews.com completely rebranded its website and dropped all of those student blogs they once featured prominently. All my blogs were gone.

Always make sure to back up your work. Even when you have a blog, do not assume it will always be there when you want to retrieve it.

I learned that lesson the hard way, but later I overcame my difficulties with not being able to start "writing a book" from scratch. Instead of sitting in front of a blank screen, I built a foundation for my books by recording my voice speaking about what I want to write. Afterward, I had the recordings converted into transcripts. It was a game-changer for me. My writing process was forever changed for the better.

CHAPTER 3

How to Dictate Your Book

You may not be the most tech-savvy individual. You might be reading this book and think, "All these tips might be great, but at the end of the day, I'm just a pen-and-paper type of person."

The most comfortable writing style for you may be pen and paper. I understand this could also be the fastest way for you to write a novel, especially if your keyboarding skills are less than fantastic.

I can understand and appreciate all of that, but if you keep things digital, it will probably be in your best interest moving forward. This is because the next step in the self-publishing workflow (after the manuscript is written) will be submitting a digital version of your work to KDP.

For this reason, I do not recommend writing things out by hand if you anticipate self-publishing your book because it will cost you excessive amounts of time in the end. I know it's tempting to go to your local Starbucks (especially if it's on the beach or up in the mountains somewhere beautiful) and write the day away in your notebook.

It's tempting as that inspiration strikes to write it all out on paper, but for the sake of your most efficient workflow, you should try to always use a word processing software like Microsoft Word.

If you're not a fast keyboarder, or you're finding it difficult to stare at a blank screen and start writing from scratch, there's a strategy I want you to consider.

The beginning stages of my writing process involves dictating out what I want to write by speaking into a microphone. Later, I have these audio recordings transcribed, and then the fun begins! I go through the transcripts and drastically re-write and edit everything.

It's not easy, but for me, it's *easier* than starting from scratch.

This is the process that has allowed me to publish three different books in the span of two years.

Yes, I am a writer by trade, and I love it more than just about anything, but I have a full-time job too. It's not always easy to find any sliver of extra time.

In addition to a full-time gig, I work as a consultant, helping clients with their communication goals and strategies, plus I produce and edit my own bi-weekly podcast—shout out to the "Characters of Boxing Podcast." I update this podcast on a regular basis in addition to my other priorities.

To make all this happen, I've set priorities as to what I want to accomplish as a writer, and I stick with it.

On a side note, I will also mention that with a consistent effort, the work feels less daunting. I work hard to get to times when I can let my guard down and relax. Since I've worked so hard to get to those "moments of relaxation," they are very palpable, and I savor them.

Writing books is a hugely important priority for me. While I don't have kids, I still know that it is possible to write no matter how busy you are. It's just a matter of taking an honest look at what you have on your plate and identifying the top priorities. If writing this book is a top priority, you will find the time.

The top priorities should include the things you do not have to do but will make you happiest. As a writer, I find publishing my own novels to be one of the top priorities in my life. I make time for what is most important to me.

Sacrifice is involved. This is because prioritizing involves saying no to a lot of things that I used to say yes to. In order to write my three previous books, I had to do some serious prioritization.

After I did the prioritization, the real work started. That real work was the actual writing. Getting the words down on paper in a way that made sense to my audience. Writing my first manuscripts through a microphone became the best way I realized I could write.

Even though you might not be tech-savvy, there is a really easy way to get your novel started that doesn't involve you having to sit there with the blank piece of paper in front of you.

This was a huge breakthrough for me because that blank piece of paper was a significant mental hurdle I had to climb in order to start writing.

If you want to dictate your book's first draft, it has never been easier. You will simply download a free recording software tool called Audacity (available online).

If you're not tech-savvy enough to know how to download it, you can ask a friend or family member to help you out. It's a pretty simple process that involves searching "Audacity" on Google and executing the download. You will also want to buy a microphone that you can plug directly into your USB port on the computer. A "USB microphone" as they are known can be purchased for around $20 - $130 dollars on Amazon. You can also buy it at a retail store like Best Buy.

I prefer a cheap USB microphone because it will get the job done, and it easily plugs directly into your computer. After you've plugged it in and opened up Audacity, you will hit record and start talking out the novel that you want to write.

You might want to list a few talking points on paper for each chapter before you start recording, but nothing has to be perfect at this point. You are getting your initial thoughts down on paper; the real work starts later once you've transcribed everything. This is when you have to go back and edit it all.

This is a great starting point because once you get those words recorded, you will be a major step closer to your self-publishing goal. After the recording, you will save it as a WAV file. Make sure to save that file somewhere on your computer's directory, where it's easy to find.

After you save the file, the next step will be to go to Speechpad.com; this is a website I've found to be easiest for getting my recordings transcribed. I do not get paid for promoting this website. (I don't get paid to promote any of the tools that I discuss in this book.)

You will submit that WAV file of recording to Speechpad.com, and for about a dollar a minute, they will create accurate transcripts of what you just dictated.

After you have the transcript, you can open it up as a Microsoft Word Document (or whatever word processing software you prefer) and start tweaking it. You can add and take out significant content. However, what you spoke into the microphone is most likely going to be the essence of your future book.

I've found this to be the best starting point for writing a book. It was through this system I was able to publish three books in one year. This was accomplished while having a full-time job, in addition to all the other crucial responsibilities that comes with living a productive adult life!

The things that are really important to me, including writing a book, I will find time for. I had a desire to write these three books, and I created artificial deadlines inside my head that I knew I needed to abide by.

When I set a strict deadline for myself that I took seriously, it was amazing what I was able to accomplish.

If I had a weekend where there were no priorities, you better believe I was inside my office with my microphone on dictating my book's essence.

Once I had the transcripts, it was time to crack open my laptop computer and re-write everything! I brought my laptop computer with me everywhere I went, whenever there was a free minute, I was writing away. It didn't matter if I was flying, taking a train, or waiting for a haircut! I was writing my book.

It is important to remember that the technical side of dictating your copy is pretty straightforward as long as you can record memos on your smartphone or download free software called Audacity, plug in a microphone to the USB port, and record what you're saying.

After that, you will save/export that file and send it over to Speechpad.com. They will provide you with the transcripts, and that will give you the head start to get your book moving.

The real art of this is deciding about what you're going to talk about into the microphone during your dictation.

Before I turn on the microphone, I have outlined everything I want to talk about in the portion of the book I am recording on that day. To do this, I go through my notes, and I bullet out the top things that I want to talk about for that particular day. (I typically do not record more than one chapter per day, or I will get burned out.)

I was taught in a speech class in eighth grade by my teacher, Mr. Jim Wainwright, that when giving a speech and preparing your notes, you never want to write things out verbatim. List out the concepts, but never write it out verbatim. Allow yourself the room for some minor improvisation during your speech. Mr. Wainwright was a great teacher, and those lessons have stuck with me to this day.

It's the most effective advice I've ever received for how best to prepare for a speaking engagement.

I look at writing a chapter in a book through dictating it, no different. I bullet out the most salient things I want to talk about, and it flows well that way as I dictate my book's chapters.

You want to allow yourself some room for improvisation and thinking on your feet. Bulleting out a few topics to talk about will allow yourself to discuss interesting key facts that pop into your head at the last minute. This will add some extra life to your final product.

Dictating your copy by speech is effective because it allows you to write in the same voice you use in everyday life. According to legendary author Kurt Vonnegut, there's nothing more powerful in writing than using your own voice and being yourself.

I know through the feedback I've received on my books that my writing tone tends to be very conversational. I try to use plain language because I want you to be able to understand what I'm saying no matter what.

There's nothing more important to me than having my audience be able to understand what I'm saying! It seems simple, but folks lose sight of this sometimes.

Vonnegut also says that readers have a difficult job. It's not easy to sit there, especially with how many distractions we have in this life, and try to understand a novel.

With this in mind, you have to write for your audience in the most inviting way possible if you want to retain them as readers.

It's not condescending to your readers to speak in a normal tone of voice to them. You don't have to try to sound like you're the greatest orator of a generation. Just be yourself. Kurt Vonnegut grew up in Indianapolis, and he says that his number one influence was the language that he heard when he was a kid in Indiana.

If you pay attention close enough, his writing will come off as a normal guy from Indianapolis. The point is that it's going to be most effective to talk in the tone of voice that best fits you. Your unique voice is something important that you bring to the table, so make it shine.

Remember, you are most likely writing to inform, but you also want to have some level of entertainment to what you're bringing to the audience. It's their choice to read your book. You want to do your reader a favor and make sure they're enjoying their time with your written material.

You will sound your most natural when you are simply dictating your book's copy in your own voice.

As I've mentioned before, the real work begins once you get those transcripts back. I've had to almost completely start from scratch on written material that I've dictated on more than one occasion. That can be the reality of it. It's easier for me to look at something that I've dictated that's bad and fix it, than look at a blank piece of paper and try to start writing from scratch.

The more comfortable you get using the combination of Audacity and a microphone to record your novels, the easier it's going to get.

The first book I ever wrote by far took me the longest time to complete. I had to learn all the steps from the beginning, but I was very patient. I avoided getting flustered when something didn't make sense.

I read message boards and watched YouTube videos about how to use the software I needed to publish my book. I took diligent notes.

When it comes to book editors, you will want to find someone to copy-edit your book for grammatical errors and sentence structure AND someone to examine the actual subject matter. If you have friends that will do it for free, that's always the best place to start. However, hiring someone to do it for you can be quite affordable in this super-competitive market of freelance talent.

Once I found my rhythm for getting the book dictated and becoming more comfortable with using Audacity to record it, the more confident I grew with the process.

That's why I want to stress the importance of being resilient in this process (especially if it's your first book.)

If you don't want to learn how to use Audacity and you have a smartphone, you have another option.

There are plenty of different voice recording apps available on smartphones. I would recommend using the Voice Memos app on the iPhone, or something similar if you have an Android device.

It might be a lot easier for you than using Audacity because the workflow is a little less complicated. You would just sit there on your iPhone, record it, and then make sure you find a way to get that recording on your iPhone over to a website such as Speechpad.com, where they will transcribe everything for you.

There are plenty of options (other than using Audacity) to record your books.

Find the way that is easiest for you. You don't have to spend money on a microphone either. I just prefer to use a USB microphone because I have gotten used to the muscle memory of holding it when I write.

It makes me feel more comfortable to be writing with this microphone in my hand. We all have our habits and creature comforts! Finding a comfortable routine as a writer is no different. Find out whatever system of recording a novel by voice is going to work best for you.

If you use the Voice Memos app on your iPhone, which is the most popular app it has for recording, the app is going to export your files in an M4A format.

You can send that M4A file directly to Speechpad.com and have it transcribed for about a dollar per minute.

A final alternative for getting transcripts of your recordings is going to take more work, but save you money. If you don't want to use a paid service like Speechpad.com, you can use the "dictate function" on Microsoft Word (the most popular word processing software on the market).

The newest versions of Microsoft Word allow you to speak directly into your microphone and have those words automatically transcribed into the document.

As you speak, it types!

It's not very accurate, so you will have to go back and rewrite a lot of what you spoke and add punctuation and paragraph breaks. The good news is that if you already have a newer version of Microsoft Word, with the dictate function, it will not cost you any extra money.

Keep in mind that Microsoft Word's dictate function is much more inaccurate than a paid service, such as Speechpad.com, so it will ultimately take you more time. Free is free, though.

If you don't want to dictate or speak your novel, and typing directly is best for you, then you can ignore this chapter.

If you need to write things out by hand, you can do that with a pen and paper, but you will have to have that written material converted into a digital format at some point. Would you be willing to pay someone to take the time to type out all your handwritten notes into a Microsoft Word document? That's the type of investment you'll need to make if you're set on writing the novel by hand.

Whatever method works best for you is the most important route to go with. I prefer to speak my words into a microphone first, as this was the way I was able to publish three books in two years.

It took a lot of hard work, dedication, and discipline, but it might just be the method that will work best for you too.

CHAPTER 4

Traditional Publishing vs. Non-Traditional

The world of traditional, or legacy publishing, is a bit complicated. It's like a private club. It's not a public golf course. It's for those that are connected or have access. Perhaps I sound a bit bitter here, but this is the most appropriate metaphor that came to mind.

Traditional publishing is an exclusive country club. Perhaps it is one that is a bit outdated and not nearly as shiny and alluring as it once was in its heyday. Meanwhile, self-publishing is the cool, new public course that just opened down the street. It might take a lot of work to "play a good round" there, but it's open to the public, so at least you'll have the opportunity.

Up until the launch of these self-publishing platforms, traditional publishing was the only option. There's no question that there are still a lot of benefits to going that route. However, I don't think most people, given what the number one disadvantage is of using a traditional publisher, will be able to go that route.

You have to understand that traditional publishing is not open to everyone. Not everyone can just wake up tomorrow and publish their book that way.

On the opposite end of the spectrum, non-traditional publishing, and its top platform, Amazon Direct Publishing (KDP), will allow anybody with a great idea a chance to publish their book. The great hockey player Wayne Gretzky once said, "I skate to where the puck is going to be, not where it has been."

I think it's fairly obvious that the future isn't going to be in traditional publishing. If we are to look at where the puck is going, then I would say self-publishing is the future.

Roughly speaking, there is very little room for profit margins in the traditional publishing world. When you look at the reality of what a first-time author brings to the table, traditional publishing has some strong benefits, but those benefits also coincide with more financial overhead. This overhead makes it more difficult for companies to make money on traditional publishing, and take a chance on a first-time author.

Established companies in creative media are typically very risk-averse. Have you ever wondered why the movie studios continue to pump money into comic book movies and sequels? These are proven viable products. The studios that produce movies are risk-averse; they are hesitant to take a chance on an original script, idea, or writer.

The same logic seems to apply in the world of traditional book publishing.

Personally, I have never gone the traditional publishing route. However, to be completely objective with you, I'm not bitter about that. There's little question that in this "digital-first" world, traditional publishing will only continue to shrink, and self-publishing will flourish.

Think about it logically. Most people are going to buy their books on Amazon (or the Kindle Store) these days. Being able to publish your own book (skip all the red tape of working with a traditional publisher) and directly sell it on Amazon, one of the largest e-commerce engines in the world is very alluring.

Amazon is a place where millions upon billions will get a chance to buy your book.

From a business perspective, self-publishing has disrupted the traditional book publishing industry in the same way the internet disrupted the newspaper industry.

However, I will admit there are good things about going the traditional publishing route.

In traditional publishing, you will (at least ostensibly) have a team dedicated to you. This team is dedicated to copy-editing your material. They will be on the front lines for you and your book, and they will be fact-checking your writing.

This reminds me again to emphasize the level of personal responsibility involved with self-publishing. You may have to hire people to copy-edit and fact check items for you. A fact-checker isn't always necessary, especially if you write fiction, but if you are writing about history (or a nonfiction account of something), then it may be wise.

When you go the traditional publishing route, a lot of that onus and responsibility will be taken off your shoulders. The traditional publishers will make sure your book's cover design is appealing, and they'll lay out the book's inside matter for you too. They'll most likely even take care of a lot of the marketing for you.

With that in mind, you can hire freelance talent on websites like Upwork.com and Fivver.com to help you with just about everything that a traditional publisher provides for you if you self-publish.

There are clearly major advantages to what a traditional publisher, and their team, brings to the picture. However, I must remind you that these services come with a cost.

You will most likely get an advance to write a book with a traditional publisher, and that advance will help pay for your daily living costs as you write the book. That advance, sometimes referred to as a *draw*, is something you will have to pay back. It's usually built-in that you pay it off through future book royalties.

This is a huge benefit because you're able to concentrate on writing your book and not necessarily worry about carrying a full-time job. Yes, that's really important, but remember, it's very difficult to get an advance because it's very difficult to do business with a traditional publisher as a first-time author.

You have to make connections, network, know the right people, and make a pitch with an airtight proposal as to why this traditional publisher should take a chance on you.

With an advance, you will not get as many royalties per copy of a book sold with a traditional publisher as you will with self-publishing. Generally, this means that as your book increases in popularity, you will see a direct increase in your royalties with self-publishing more than you will with traditional publishers.

Traditional publishers will typically have the connections and infrastructure to get the physical copy of your book for sale in different bookstores. This is fading as a valuable benefit, simply because there are less and less brick and mortar bookstores and retailers out there.

I love a good bookstore, nothing beats strolling around a bookstore. However, our market-based society is proving that it's harder and harder for bookstores to keep up with paying their rents and making a profit. This is because of things like Amazon's nimble delivery methods for book publishing.

With that in mind, the connections that these traditional book publishers have with brick and mortar distribution outlets are not nearly as important as they used to be. That is because Amazon is king.

Amazon is where so many people find just about anything to buy. If you get your book on Amazon's marketplace, it could catch positive momentum because people are going to be seeing it a lot, given their robust search engine.

With Amazon, there's a chance your book will organically get many good reviews, and then it'll all snowball for you in a positive way. The next thing you know, you may be selling books left and right even though you didn't use a traditional publisher.

I also want to make it clear that a traditionally published book will also be on Amazon too, please note that Amazon is not just a marketplace for those that self-publish. With a traditional book publisher, the book you sell on Amazon will have to deal with all the other financial overheads, though. This means that in general, the royalties you'll get from selling your book on Amazon with a traditional publisher will not be as fruitful as they will be with self-publishing it.

If you opt for the non-traditional route, Amazon and BarnesandNoble.com both provide a state of the art on-demand publishing infrastructure.

Please note that if you used Barnes and Noble's online self-publishing resource (https://press.barnesandnoble.com/), your book would not automatically be available in their brick and mortar stores. It is simply a competitor to Amazon's KDP and allows folks to buy your book through BarnesAndNoble.com.

With these self-publishing tools, you don't have to worry about having excessive book inventory.

If you go the traditional book-publishing route, there might be a situation where you get a bunch of copies of your book that you're going to have to put into storage. You might have to keep boxes of storage in your basement/garage, and they could simply go to waste. With Amazon's publishing on-demand infrastructure, you'll never have to deal with any wasteful inventory because books are only published after they are ordered.

Another advantage of going the non-traditional, self-publishing route is the fact that you are the boss, and you are ultimately in control of the story. You have the final say in all editorial decisions.

If you're going the traditional book publishing route, of course, the people who are publishing this book for you are going to have the final say. It's important to know you are the boss with non-traditional publishing, but with traditional publishing, you will not be the boss—especially as a first-time author.

When it comes to self-publishing on Amazon, there is a small gatekeeping process where your book has to get approved before it's officially available on Amazon. However, this approval process almost becomes a formality as long as there is no hate speech or anything that's really egregiously wrong with your book.

(Amazon also will want to make sure you don't have any technical errors, but this is something we'll discuss in the next chapter.)

Plagiarism will also get your book flagged and taken down from Amazon, but of course, that should not be a problem with your first book, because we're all adults here.

Another thing I love about non-traditional publishing is that you don't have to wait around for approval from a traditional publisher. You can get actionable on self-publishing a book today with Amazon or with Barnes & Noble's self-publishing platforms. You don't have to worry about politicking anyone.

You don't have to stress out about setting up a meeting with someone at a traditional book publishing office. There's no need to worry about greasing any wheels, brown-nosing, or doing anything uncomfortable politically to get your book published. Think of all that energy you will save! Use that extra energy to make your book even better!

Saving energy is huge, and that's a really important thing to underscore because we all have a finite amount of energy. That energy (and of course time) you are spending trying to court a traditional publisher could be better spent writing your novel.

The world of traditional publishing is simply not open to everyone.

This is a major deal-breaker for many people. Either way, I urge you to be strong-willed and persistent. No matter what route you go to get your book published, you will need to have thick skin.

Trying to curry favor with a traditional book publisher will burn calories, and if you're spending finite energy trying to get in the door at a book publisher, you're going to find yourself with a lot of limited energy left to write the actual book.

However, just to play devil's advocate and be fully transparent, I will note that if you do land a deal with a traditional publisher, then you will get a chance at earning a book advance. That advance will allow you to not worry as much financially about your day-to-day responsibilities because you'll be able to pay for some of your daily expenses with it. With an advance, you won't necessarily have to have a full-time job like you would with non-traditional publishing. This would ultimately save you energy, at least in theory.

Please realize that getting the word out about your book is a difficult process. Marketing your book is so different than writing it. Marketing is not a skill inherent to most authors.

Thus, I will admit that a traditional publisher will give you a chance to market your book a little bit better, and this could help you. However, there are some simple ways to market your self-published book that I'll discuss later.

Identify why you're writing this book before you make your final decision about what type of publishing route you will pursue. Is this book for your family (and future generations) so they can have a legacy of you? Well, then you probably don't have to worry too much about marketing it to the general public.

Is this book for strangers? Do you want the general public to stumble upon it on Amazon and get a chance to read about your beautiful idea or story? Then you really need to sink more resources and efforts into marketing, and that is where a traditional publisher will be able to lead the way for you.

Be honest with yourself.

A traditional publisher can take that marketing burden off you a bit, but someone willing to go through the entire process of writing a book can learn some stress-free marketing tricks.

All of us probably know how to send an email here. Your marketing needs may be as simple as gathering a bunch of emails of people who know and love you and spreading the news about your book's availability that way. Emailing people is probably the easiest way to market your book. You can do that without the marketing muscle that a traditional publisher will offer you.

The reason I have always opted to self-publish is that there is no gatekeeper. I can start writing my future book today. No red tape. No relationship building needed. Just writing!

Deciding to go the self-publishing route was an easy decision for me, and probably will be for you too. If you really want to do this without any political hurdles, then go with the self-publishing option.

Some of the benefits of traditional publishing have eroded in our digital times. This includes the readily available surplus of freelance labor that can help edit your copy and design your book's artwork.

You will hire these people on an on-demand basis. You won't have to spend a lot either with them, because the rates on these websites (Fiverr.com, Upwork.com, etc.) are very competitive. There are no scams here as these are the best rates available. The only thing you have to do is make sure the freelancer you're about to hire has a lot of positive reviews before you pay them.

Don't avoid self-publishing because you are intimidated by having to learn a couple of tricks with the technology of the Kindle Direct Publishing platform. As I'll explain in the next chapter, there is nothing to fear with "mastering" this self-publishing format.

When it comes to any of these self-publishing technologies, there are many freelancers available to help you with any task along the journey!

CHAPTER 5

Kindle Direct Publishing

Don't let the name fool you. The Kindle Direct Publishing (KDP) self-publishing platform is for more than just Kindle books. It is the same platform where you will self-publish your paperback.

By now, you are probably familiar with the concept of an e-reader. It's a portable device that can hold thousands of books with the added benefit of being extremely low weight. (This is unlike traditional books that remind you how heavy they are on moving day).

Amazon's e-reader is called the Kindle. If you decide to self-publish a book, with a few extra steps and clicks, you can have your book available in the No. 1 book-selling directory (Amazon) as both a Kindle product and paperback.

When Amazon launched this platform in 2007, they were also launching the Kindle. As a result, the entire self-publishing platform has been branded as Kindle Direct Publishing (KDP). Despite the name, I've been able to get far more out of this platform, in terms of selling books, by utilizing the paperback printing on-demand service.

I've sold Kindle books too, but I've grown my readership far more by selling paperbacks.

KDP is where you upload your entire book's contents, set the price, receive revenues, etc. It's a hub for all of that. When you successfully upload a book through KDP, it can be approved in a couple of days and then available to the world on Amazon.com.

Before getting started with KDP, I do recommend you get your book's cover designed by a professional or friend, someone who knows what they're doing.

You can find someone to do this for you on Fiverr.com or Upwork.com.

After you have your book written in Microsoft Word (or whatever word processing file you've saved it as), you can submit that file to a freelancer on Fiverr or Upwork and request that they format your manuscript for you, so it's ready for KDP.

To find a freelance artist to help you do this, go to Fiverr.com and type "Layout a book for KDP" in the search bar, then click enter.

For a fee from roughly $10 to $40, someone should be able to do this for you. (You can also format your book using a template from KDP if you feel confident enough. KDP will give a Microsoft Word template for free to you that you will paste your text into. However, it might be easier to let a professional do this for you, if it's your first time publishing a book on KDP.)

After your manuscript is ready for print, I recommend that you use Fiverr to have your book cover designed.

Simply search "Design my Book's Cover for KDP" in the search bar within Fiverr.com, and you will get many search results of folks that can help you. I will estimate that you can expect to spend $30 - $50 for a quality book cover design. Choose your freelance artist based on how many positive reviews they have on Fiverr.

When you communicate with your Fiverr freelance artist about what your book is about, they can create the best possible book cover for you. Let them know you want your book to stand out on Amazon. Request them to use a bold color palette, and let them know you don't want them to use more than two or three colors, so the cover doesn't look too crowded.

You'll need to tell the freelancer what the book is about, so provide them with a brief description and let them know who the intended audience will be.

It's important that you tell them how many pages your book is, so they know how wide to make the width of the book's spine. I encourage you to go with cream paper (instead of white paper). The old rule of thumb with cream paper:

(page count) x 0.0025" = the width of your book cover's spine

Make sure you tell the freelancer the exact title, subtitle (if you have a subtitle), and spelling of the author's name.

Ask your freelance artist to leave room for the barcode on the book's back cover. (KDP will automatically add a barcode to the back of your book later). The freelance website where you hire your cover artist will require that you communicate things like this to the artist. It will automatically prompt you to enter anything you would like to communicate to them when you purchase their services.

Tell the freelance designer that the back cover of the book should include a brief description of your book, and a section for an *About the Author* section. Here is what I requested for a recent book:

Description (100-150 words): *This book is about how (and why) to get tactical with the various tools of altmetrics—Twitter, Facebook for Business, YouTube, Podcasting, Kindle Direct Publishing, and much more—to bolster the reach of all the hard work that you are a part of in academia.*

These tools help ensure your work and research will be seen by more people, and maybe even increase the likelihood of acquiring more funding for your research. It takes more than just knowledge about

how to use these tools to truly get the most of them—you must carefully strategize and plan what you want to say, and when you are going to say it, as this book thoroughly describes.

This book could be a key element in furthering your career in academia and increasing the value you bring to society. It'll help open your horizons in communications and make your work more accessible and comprehendible to a much larger audience.

About the Author (75 – 100 words): *Casey Callanan, MBA, is the owner of Clear Contender Media, a company he started to further his life goals of helping the world communicate better. As a lifelong writer and boxing enthusiast, he believes the same principles that make a great prizefighter (perseverance, resilience, and the will to be great) translate perfectly to the world of communications. As a successful podcast host with a background in journalism and digital marketing, he's in the business of helping people communicate better one story at a time. He is also the author of* How to Podcast When You Aren't Tech Savvy.

I also requested that they add the following copy to my book's spine:

The spine of the book should contain the words: Altmetrics for Academic Faculty

I provided a high-resolution headshot digital photograph of myself for the artist to add to the back cover of the book. This is optional, though. You definitely do not need a photo of yourself for the book.

The freelance artist will send you a version of the book's cover within a week or so after you request it. This is a very exciting time. I always look forward to opening the email and seeing what my new cover will look like!

Once you have a manuscript and book cover secured, you are ready to rock and roll. It's time to get on KDP's website and apply to have your book sold on Amazon!

KDP is a remarkable tool. Now let's dive into how to get started with it.

First, you will open up your favorite web browser. Inside the browser, you will paste the web address:

http://kdp.amazon.com/

…into your browser's address bar (this is the bar at the top of your browser where web addresses appear as you search the web).

Once you enter KDP's website, you will be asked to sign in. If you already have an Amazon account, use the same username and password that you use to sign in to Amazon when you go shopping. If you don't already have an Amazon account, then you will be asked to create a new username and password.

After you sign in, you should see the words *Create a New Title*. Nearby those words, you should see two options. One option will allow you to *Add a Kindle eBook,* and another will allow you to *Add a Paperback.*

I recommend that you add your paperback first, so click on that option.

The first page will have you add your paperback's details. Many of these items will be obvious and self-explanatory, such as entering what language it is, your name, publishing rights (either you own the rights to the book or you don't; unless you are doing something super unorthodox—you own the rights), and whether or not it contains adult content.

Some of the trickier items that might take a little more thought include:

- Your book's subtitle (your book will obviously need to have a title, but a subtitle is optional).
- Entering your book's serial number and the edition number is optional. (I've never used this feature, and any first-time author should probably ignore this field for now; you can always go back and adjust this later.)
- If you had a major co-author or illustrator, you would want to add it under the *Contributors* field. I would only add a contributor in this field if they played a major role in this book's editorial development. You can always acknowledge folks inside your book's front matter before the first chapter begins.
- Categories are also important. This is how Amazon will categorize your book. Select a category that best describes the subject matter of your book. This should be fairly obvious, just make sure to take your time and add the book's category here. You are allowed to add two different categories, so take advantage and add it to both.
- Keywords are important for how people find you on Amazon. Essentially, you'll want to add short

phrases or words that reflect what your book is about. Try to put yourself in the shoes of someone that's searching for what your book is about. What keywords would they enter in Amazon to try to find it? Keywords are important if you are looking to sell your book and have it found organically. Make sure to read more about what goes into a strong keyword within KDP's robust Help Center. There is an informative section about this within these webpages. The URL to access this help section is: https://kdp.amazon.com/en_US/help/

Next, you will save these changes and continue to the section where you enter your paperback's contents. This is where things will get a little more technical.

I want you to get your book into Amazon, and having that done is always better than chasing perfection. With this in mind, I'll offer you my recommendations for how to get through this section without losing years of your life, splitting hairs, and drowning in the potential minutiae.

The International Standard Book Number (ISBN) is essentially a serial number for your book. Simply request a KDP ISBN number at this point of loading your book's contents, and they will give it to you for free!

You can enter your book's publication date next. I would just enter whatever the current day is here. This will eventually show up on Amazon to inform potential buyers when your book was published.

Next, you'll need to enter a series of questions about the book's physical characteristics. If you are writing a paperback that is entirely text, you will be able to do this quite easily.

If you are writing a book that is chock full of illustrations, it will take additional research to ensure your illustrations aren't compromised during the layout and production of your physical book.

If you want a hardcover book, KDP will not be an option for you. I recommend trying to use the Barnes and Noble self-publishing platform for this. It is available at https://press.barnesandnoble.com/

If your paperback is mostly text, then I recommend you go with the following:

Interior & paper type: Black & White Interior with Cream Paper

Trim Size: 6x9 inches

Bleed Settings: No Bleed

Paperback cover finish: Matte

Next, you will upload the manuscript and book cover. Doing this should come after your book has been copy-edited and fully laid out properly. A professional should have already designed the book's cover for you before you upload this final version of it.

You will now be asked by KDP to review a final version of what your book and cover will look like. If Amazon doesn't find any technical errors with your manuscript and book cover, then it is time to move on to naming a price for your book!

The final section of KDP, before it's time to apply to have it sold on Amazon, involves setting a price. Let's be honest; you are a first-time author, so have a conservative price for your book. I recommend (depending on how long it is) setting a price at around $5.99 - $8.99 for a first-time author.

You will get a royalty for roughly 2 or 3 dollars for each book sold. That's pretty decent, considering you are a first-time author!

When KDP asks you to "Select the territories for which you hold distribution rights," I recommend that you select **All Territories (Worldwide Rights)**, and when it asks you to allow **Expanded Distributed**, check *yes*. Having expanded distribution simply means more countries will be able to purchase your book at no additional cost to you. KDP is a wonderful tool!

After your book is successfully submitted to Amazon, it will take a couple of days for Amazon to email you about whether your book was accepted or rejected.

If it was rejected, it most likely means there was something wrong with the way your book's manuscript or cover was formatted. This is a good time to contact the freelancer who worked on your manuscript or cover. Copy/paste the email that you got from Amazon explaining why your book was rejected and send that to the freelance artist who worked on your book.

They will most likely fix the issue for free since it was probably their error in the first place. If they do not cooperate with you, you can issue a complaint about it on Fiverr or Upwork.

If you use a professional with many positive reviews on Fiverr and Upwork, you most likely will not have any issues, and they will be happy to help you. When you pay people to work on your book, they should function (within reason) as an extended member of your team!

Your team's collective goal is to get a book published on Amazon.

If your book is accepted by Amazon, you can order *Author Copies* of your book (so you don't have to pay the full amount that your book will cost the public on Amazon). Amazon will allow you to buy up to 999 copies of your own book at the cost it takes Amazon to publish it (plus shipping).

To order Author Copies of your book, you will simply do the following:

- First, you will open up your web browser and enter the following URL into it: https://kdp.amazon.com/
- When you are on this page, you will click on the button that says, "Sign In with Your Amazon Account."
- Next, there will be a screen for you to sign in. It will say, "Sign in With Your Amazon login."
- Enter your Email and Password.

- Now you will be logged-in to your Author's Account Profile Page. On the bottom right-hand corner of the screen, you will see the words "PAPERBACK ACTIONS" and below that there will be a button that says "PROMOTE & ADVERTISE."
- You will hover your mouse over the small button with three dots on it to the right of where it says "PROMOTE & ADVERTISE."
- After you hover your mouse over that small button with the three dots on it, one of the options will appear that says "Request Author Copies" (click on that option).
- After you click on "Request Author Copies," the next screen will have you enter how many copies you want. It will also have you select the "Marketplace of your Order." Select the "Marketplace of your Order" as *Amazon.com* (or whatever marketplace best coincides with the country you live in) from the dropdown menu.
- Next, you will click "Submit Order."
- After you hit "Submit Order," you will then be taken to your normal Amazon Shopping Cart, and you'll check out as you normally would while using Amazon.

For a few more additional steps, you can also have your book added to Amazon.com as a Kindle version as well. To add a Kindle version of your book, you visit the same URL that you used to add the paperback version of your book: https://kdp.amazon.com/en_US/bookshelf

This time, underneath where it says *Create a New Title,* click on the plus sign where it says *Kindle eBook.*

The steps to add a Kindle eBook are very similar to adding a paperback title. The main difference is the cover for the Kindle version will be a different size than your paperback cover. The price for a Kindle version of your book should be less than what you would charge for a paperback. (You will still get a royalty on Kindle sales, but it's less than a paperback royalty.)

To get a cover for your Kindle book, I recommend once again leaning on the freelance artist who created your paperback cover. This is because the dimensions of a Kindle book cover are different from a paperback.

If you search, *Convert my paperback cover to a KDP Kindle Version* in the search bar of Fiverr.com or Upwork.com (reliable freelance labor websites), you will find someone who can create this for you based on your paperback's cover.

Also, keep in mind that you don't NEED a Kindle version of your book. Sometimes just having a paperback version of your first book is enough. With that in mind, feel free to skip the steps it takes to create the Kindle-version of your book if you feel overwhelmed by the additional task.

CHAPTER 6

The Audio Version of Your Book

There are plenty of great reasons to record an audio version of your book. You can record your "book on tape" on your own, or you can hire someone to do it for you. It all depends on how comfortable you are with learning how to record your own audio if you don't know how to do it.

Recording your book's contents is a painless process that involves a USB microphone. I vouch for the use of a USB microphone as it's the easiest way to record quality audio with your computer.

Using a USB microphone allows you to make sure the audio attains a good enough quality to be accepted as an audiobook. You don't need a recording studio either, an enclosed quiet space (i.e., a walk-in closet) could do the trick for you.

A USB microphone can range from $20 - $200. I would recommend spending $50 - $70 on the *Blue Snowball USB Microphone* to get the job done for you. Simply search *Blue Snowball USB Microphone* in Amazon or Walmart.com, and it should pop up as an option for you to buy.

With an audio version of your book, you could actually apply to have your book sold on Audible. This is an Amazon-owned service that distributes audiobooks. It's another avenue for audiences to consume your story.

It's always better to have multiple ways for folks to consume your book. An audio version of your book brings with it more visibility for you as an author. Remember, it is not necessary to have an audio version of your book. It's a luxury.

Creating the audio version of your book should not impede your ability to finish your print book. This is because the work comes after your book has already been created. The audio version of the book is simply icing on the cake, so to speak.

It's more of a marketing opportunity, and because it does not serve as an extra hurdle for you in the process of getting the book done, I really like it.

There are so many extra hurdles that can sidetrack you during the actual production of your book, so you should be on heightened alert as to where you can save time/energy. In theory, this task comes afterward. (With that in mind, please do not take this task on, or even burn calories thinking about it, until the paperback version of your book is completely done.)

When the proper time comes, I recommend taking advantage of creating the audio version of your book, though, because there are benefits, and it shouldn't cost you a lot of money to make it a reality.

If you're not tech-savvy enough to learn how to record the audio version of your book on your own, it will obviously cost a bit more money. This is because you'll want to hire a freelance voiceover artist to record it for you.

You may also want to consider hiring a freelance voiceover artist to record the audio version of your book if you don't think your voice is good enough to take on the task! You don't have to sound like a BBC broadcast anchor to record an audio version of your book, but you should be self-aware of your limitations. Some people have to be honest with themselves and realize their voice is not professional enough sounding to do it on their own.

It's easy to hire freelance voiceover artists by using websites such as Upwork.com, Fiverr.com, Voices.com, and Voices123.com.

On the other hand, it's still my firm belief that there's nothing like having an author read their own book. In my view, it's the best way to have an audio version of your book done right. Nobody knows the content of the book better than the author, and no one can have the proper inflections in their voice as accurately as the book's original author.

With that in mind, I do encourage you to produce the audio version of your book on your own, but I understand if it's something you're not interested in sinking your energy into.

The benefits of having an audio version of your book, include:

- Opportunities to make extra revenue.
- Increasing the amount of free things you can give away to build your credibility as an author.
- Growing the amount of ways people can consume your stories.
- Being more inclusive and accessible.

It's always good to make extra revenue, and perhaps it can offset some of the other monetary costs you've incurred to create and market this book. Increasing the amount of free things you can give away with your book is important if you are networking with people and looking to establish your expertise on a certain subject.

Say you are trying to get your next book distributed/published through a traditional publishing company. You will want to build some credibility with this book publisher down the line as you are trying to impress them.

You also want to give them every opportunity possible to consume your book's manuscript. Maybe they do not have the time to sit down and read a manuscript, but they may have the bandwidth to listen to an audio version of your book on their way to work.

They could listen while they're at the gym and walking their dog every night. Having an audio version of your book is really important because now more than ever, people are consuming books with their smartphone and headphones on the go. There is an influx of great audio content to consume right now, and apps like Audible are leading this charge.

People seem like they have less time than ever with the demands of today's economy and life. It's also no secret that time becomes more valuable as you are trying to raise children.

Busy professionals like to think they don't have extra time to sit and read every day. As a workaround, people are consuming audio more and more because of how portable it is.

Some say we are in the second coming of a golden age of audio. We had the golden age of audio when the radio boom was taking off in the 20th century, but now it seems like people are coming back to audio. It's an enjoyable, timeless way to deliver storytelling.

Having an audio version of your book gives you a chance to keep up with the times.

There are also some networking advantages with an audio version of your book that I want you to consider.

Networking is an art (far from an exact science), so there are many variables involved. However, I think a good tool to have in your back pocket is a book that establishes you as an expert on a certain subject.

If people start talking about podcasting during a networking event, and you wrote a book about podcasting, then it might be a good time to bring that up! Furthermore, you can offer to send the person you are networking with a free copy of your book as a PDF or MP3 file so they can listen or read it later.

More times than not, if you're sending someone a PDF version or MP3 file (audio version) of your book, they're going to be happy to get something for free. They're going to be excited about it. Why not make that networking opportunity even sweeter and tell someone you'll email them the audio version of your book along with a free PDF of it?

It's going to make you seem that much more credible, plus it is impressive when you can provide an audio file and PDF of your book to someone for free. We all love free!

There is no real overhead with doing that. This is because you will email them the audio file and of your book, and you will not have to deal with shipping costs.

If you never create an audio version of your book, you can also just send them a PDF of your book instead. (Creating a PDF is easy, you just save the Microsoft Word version of your finalized manuscript as a PDF file. Later you can email that PDF file to whomever you like. If you can't figure it out, just send them the book as a Microsoft Word file.)

It's also a good idea to create an audio version of your book if you plan to get even more creative down the line and sell something like a course to go along with your book. This is great if your book is nonfiction, and you are trying to teach something with your book.

Perhaps you are teaching people how to take great photography in America's national parks. You can package the sale of that e-book with an audio version when you sell it.

You can use a free service like Thinkific.com to build a course based on your book.

It doesn't cost anything to sign up for Thinkific.com, and you can sell the audio version of your book with the course along with a series of videos that you created of lesson plans based on your book.

It would be an amazing value proposition for readers if you coupled your book with a free course you created with Thinkific.com if it's non-fiction. Maybe your book is about wildlife or land preservation; a course would go along nicely with your book.

You could certainly do this by creating a series of videos for free that you record using a webcam. If you put a lot of time and effort into the videos, you can charge people a small fee to register for the course.

Creating a course based on your book with Thinkific.com can be complex and challenging as you'll need to record lesson plans and be strategic with instructional design and course development principles. With that in mind, this may not be an option for everyone.

However, it could create a new revenue stream for your project if your book is nonfiction, and it falls into the "How to" space. Please keep in mind that not all people are that entrepreneurial, and if it's too confusing or complicated to record an audio version of your book (or course), then don't worry about it and skip these steps!

Recording a book on tape and selling it is not as hard as writing an entire book. That's why I encourage folks to take advantage of this next step when it's feasible for them.

If you do plan on creating an audio version of your book, you'll want to log into the Audiobook Creation Exchange, ACX.

ACX is the platform you will use to distribute the audio version of your book. It's similar to KDP. Just like you use KDP to upload your book so it can be sold/distributed on Amazon, you use ACX so the audio version of your book can be sold/distributed through Audible.

Audible is the No. 1 marketplace for books on tape. It is owned by Amazon.

Visit www.ACX.com to get started. You will sign-in using your Amazon account details since ACX is directly connected to Amazon.

ACX is where you can also hire voiceover talent, but you'll get much cheaper rates for hiring a voiceover artist by using Upwork.com and Fiverr.com. These two websites tend to have the lowest freelance artist rates on the internet, and this includes voiceover work.

With that in mind, I will recommend that you do not use ACX to find your voiceover talent. Instead, get the files created by using talent hired on Fiverr.com. The final step will be to then take those files back to ACX to have your audiobook created and eventually published on ACX where it will be distributed through Audible.com

Remember, Audible is a distribution outlet and app where most people are getting their audiobooks these days.

Learning ACX will require more discipline and patience to master, just like it did to use KDP.

The internet is full of credible, free advice with how to use ACX, given its robust lineup of forums, help pages (https://audible-acx.custhelp.com/), and YouTube videos. Since using it isn't completely necessary in order to get your book published, I don't want to go into every painstaking detail about how to use ACX in this book.

The bottom line is that if you want folks to have a chance to buy your book on tape, then it needs to go through ACX to get accepted into Audible.com. Audible is the largest audiobook exchange portal in the world right now.

If you don't want to hire freelance talent to read your book, then do it yourself by downloading Audacity. Audacity is a reliable, free software for recording and editing your own audio.

You don't have to be tech-savvy to start using it. Plug in a USB microphone in your computer's USB outlet and hit the record button in Audacity. You don't need a studio to record. Just make sure you're in a quiet environment, and you are speaking directly into the microphone. Take these precautions, and you should be able to get away with recording your book for free with just a USB microphone, Audacity, and a heap load of patience/willpower.

You don't have to make things more complicated than that.

Try not to spend a lot of money creating a super high-quality audio version of your book. It's harder to make up those expenses by selling audiobooks than it is selling the Kindle and paperback version of your book. If you don't plan on selling the audiobook and you're just trying to package it into an email that you plan to send to family, friends, and networking acquaintances, then feel free to record it yourself!

When you are trying to establish yourself as an expert and an author, it does take effort. Spreading the word about your book takes a desire to network with people and tell them about it any way you can.

Emailing people the audio version of your book will only help you do that. It takes work if you really want to get your book seen by many people.

Releasing your book as a free podcast is another option to consider if you have an audiobook. It's a good choice for people that simply have a goal of having their stories told (and making money isn't what drives them).

Releasing your book chapter by chapter as a podcast could be a great option for both fiction and non-fiction authors.

Fiction and "true crime" podcasts are very popular right now. This is why a podcast could be a great idea for someone who is looking to increase their book's awareness.

Creating a podcast takes some considerable extra effort. In my first book, *How to Podcast When You Aren't Tech Savvy*, I go into great detail about how to launch a podcast. Visit my website at www.ClearContender.com/Contact and send me a message. I'm happy to send you a free PDF of this book if you request it from me there!

Either way, please check that book out if you want to learn about how to get a podcast created in the simplest fashion possible.

A podcast is a great idea for increasing the visibility of your book, and each chapter of your book could be an individual podcast episode. In general, there is no limit to how long (or how short) a podcast episode needs to be!

If you go this route, your podcast can potentially reach more people than ever, and it can be a way to cross-promote the print version of your book. You could provide folks with a direct link on where they can go to purchase your paperback in the description of your episode when you post each podcast.

You could release the entire book for free as a podcast. Going this route could honestly either help or hurt your pursuit of making money from the book. It's hard to say. It could raise awareness enough to the point that people will want to also read the print version of the book, or it could result in people losing interest altogether.

However, if your goal is to get your stories heard by people, then this is a great option for you. Perhaps this is only the first book of many you plan to write, and you want to build your name as an author, then releasing this first book for free as a podcast could be a smart idea.

If your goal is just to get the book out there, there's no shame in taking advantage of giving away your book for free to everyone.

Somewhere down the line, you just never know what can happen when eyeballs reach your book.

Opportunities open up with the more people your book reaches, and that is why I always recommend you consider having an audio version of your book created.

CHAPTER 7

Promoting Your Book with a Shoestring Budget

You must set a budget before you start marketing your book. There are many different avenues for marketing your book, but the first step should always be to set a budget.

Maybe your marketing budget is $100.

There is nothing wrong with that. It's a fine place to start. While that might be a lot of money for some folks, relatively speaking, that is what I would call a shoestring budget.

If marketing your book is something that you care about and something you're willing to get creative with and work hard to do, there are plenty of free ways to market your book. The best-known way to increase a book's visibility organically is by getting its Amazon reviews up.

In the world of marketing, the word "organic" typically means free, or without having to pay for advertising.

There is an ethical way to get your Amazon reviews up, and that includes giving away the PDF version of your book for free and kindly requesting that the person visits Amazon after reading it, and gives an honest review of your book. To me, as long as you do not sway them in the direction to give you a positive review, this is ethical.

Now, you could argue that by giving someone a free version of your book, you're already swaying them in the direction of giving you a good review, but in my opinion, if you're honest with the person, there is nothing wrong with this in my view. Request they leave an honest review of what they thought about your book on Amazon. Let them know they don't have to do this.

I don't think there's anything wrong with sending a free PDF of your book to a select group of friends and family and asking them to review it honestly. I will note that I'm not a lawyer, so before you sink a lot of resources into giving out free copies of your book in exchange for asking people to review it—seek legal counsel and be aware of what the laws are in your area.

From what I gather, laws are rapidly changing in the realm of Google, Amazon, and Yelp reviews.

The most important reviews are "verified purchase" reviews on Amazon as they hold the most weight. The best way to get your book seen and to have it rank higher on the Amazon search engine is to get reviews of your book from verified purchases. This means the reviewer has a verified purchase on their profile of your book, and it will be indicated next to where they reviewed your book.

This will help you rank higher on Amazon's search engine.

We don't know the exact variables that Amazon uses to rank content on its search engine, because that is a trade secret. However, we know that the more positive reviews your book has, the higher it's going to rank. When someone searches a keyword that's related to your book, your book will show up higher and faster if it has more reviews.

Of course, the best way to guarantee you will get good reviews is to make sure your book is good in the first place! Yes, that is subjective, but doing the upfront work and research plus having multiple people copy-edit and proofread it will start to pay off when you see positive reviews of your book pop up. It is gratifying when strangers buy your book on Amazon.

It can feel brutal to be on the receiving end of a bad review, and you may need a thick skin to stomach reading a negative review. No one likes to be criticized, but if what the reviewer wrote is fair, then you have to take that advice in stride and vow to use it to make you better in the future.

If someone is downright nasty and unfair with their review—then that is a different story. Cyberbullying is a dark art and takes a lot of mental fortitude to deal with the best. For more on that topic, check out my book, *Anxiety Relief from Online Bullies: Guidance to Fight Negative Vibes and Internet Trolls.*

(Contact me by visiting www.ClearContender.com/Contact and send me a message if you have been on the receiving end of a cyberbully. I will happily send you a free PDF of this book.)

I do recommend trying to build positive reviews as the cornerstone of your marketing strategy, and to do that, you have to get your book in front of people. Word of mouth marketing may eventually be the most important way to get your book appreciated, but paid advertising will help you too.

Paid advertising is an effective way to get the ball rolling in terms of getting your book read and (hopefully) reviewed.

You can't get a review until someone has read it. So your number one priority is making sure people are reading it!

After publishing your book, write a friendly email to every friend, family member, co-worker, and acquaintance you have to spread the word about your book's release.

You can send an email to your list of friends and families, but try not to do it more than two times for each book. You don't want to create what's known as *email fatigue* with your friends and family. Email fatigue is when people get so many emails from someone that they simply don't bother reading it anymore. The communication will eventually get completely ignored.

Before you send out this email, build a spreadsheet using Microsoft Excel or Google Spreadsheets to create a list of every friend or family member in your network.

You can go on Facebook to start listing folks. Do you still have an old address book? Use it. Get creative.

List as many people as you can think of, and then try to get an email for every one of them. Ask around for email addresses. It takes hard work to do this, but again, it is free. When you have limited marketing dollars to spend, this is important to do.

It's imperative to build this email list. Now, you might be asking yourself, "Why don't I just do a Facebook post to get people aware of my book?"

Of course, you can do that, but an email is more targeted, and people are more likely to pay attention to it. We know that social media companies have algorithms where posts that you create might not be showing up on every one of your followers' feeds. This is why having a targeted email list is so important.

Facebook is a great starting place for looking at who you are friends with and seeing whose email you have. Feel free to also make a Facebook post about your new book. However, it is my firm belief that sending out a personalized email is a better place to start.

I recommend you only send two emails to this group of friends and family for each one of the books that you publish. The first email you write to them should be a month or two before the book is published.

At this point, you can "build some hype" for your book by telling everyone that a book you are about to publish is on its way soon. This should build some excitement and anticipation about your book.

When the book is finished and available on Amazon, you can send them a link to it and announce the book has been written!

I also recommend that you attach a PDF of your book in this email. Let your friends and family know your book is available to purchase, but they can also read the PDF version that you attached to the email.

Request that they please write a review on Amazon about it after reading it.

When it comes to the "free marketing" of your book, emailing friends and family is the first and easiest thing to check off your list.

If you've created the audio version of your book, send that to your friends/family for free too. Keep in mind, this file containing the audio version of your book might be big, so you might have to send it as a Dropbox link, a zip file, or from a Gmail account.

There are many ways to send large files for free. If it's too big to email out, the easiest thing to do is to send it as an attachment in an email from a Gmail account. Gmail will automatically send the file for you through Google Drive (a free cloud computing service). If you don't want to learn how to use Dropbox, just send large email files from a Gmail email account!

Gmail accounts are free, and if you don't have one, Dropbox is also free to use.

If you're noticing someone hasn't reviewed your book, don't be afraid to follow up with them and nudge them a little bit about it. I would just make sure you have a strong, existing relationship with that individual as you don't want to come off as "pushy."

You don't have to be annoying about it, but if it's your Aunt that you're very close with, then feel free to say something along the lines of:

Hi Aunt Mary,

I hope you are doing well, and I wanted to thank you again for reading my book! I noticed that you didn't review it yet though on Amazon. No biggie, but if you find the time, can you please consider doing that for me if you get a chance? I love you, and I'll see you soon!"

These are just some ideas on how to get that free marketing push without spending a lot of money. Post about your book on Facebook (like we discussed) and LinkedIn.

If you're on Twitter, send a tweet. You can't be sending tweets about this all day, every day, but if you do send a tweet about it, make it your pinned tweet. The pinned tweet is the tweet that everyone sees when they first land on your Twitter profile. A pinned tweet gets by far the most impressions of anything else on your Twitter profile.

Are you on Instagram? Then create an Instagram post with your book cover on it. I will note that at some point, you cannot solely be relying on social media.

Social media is great because it is free to post things, but be careful. Posting too much about it will fatigue your followers and friends. This could end up hurting your book's visibility as they won't want to hear about it.

I recommend having a quick YouTube video created about your book. I encourage doing this because posting to YouTube is free.

You can use your webcam. Just turn that webcam on and talk about your book. Have the book with you when you talk about it as a visual aid. Make the video brief. YouTube has a major potential reach, and it's free to create an account and upload a video. Free tools, such as these as your best bet with marketing your book on a tight budget.

Give your local library a call or visit. Find out how you can get your book in the library. It's just a matter of calling people and having these conversations. If you're not tech-savvy and you prefer talking to people, then, by all means, drive over to that bookstore near your house, and take a ride to your local library.

Talk to staff face-to-face and let them know you wrote a book. There's nothing bad that can come from these conversations.

Wasn't it Michael Jordan that said he missed 100% of the shots he didn't take?

You're at an advantage if you enjoy talking to people face-to-face. A lot of the younger generations struggle with face-to-face conversation. They might be a little socially awkward because they're so used to being behind a computer/smartphone screen all day.

If you're comfortable with talking to people face-to-face, then, by all means, take advantage of that strength you have, and drive to the local bookstore to let them know you have a new book. Politely ask them what the procedure is for getting a new book from a local author on the shelves.

These are all free marketing tactics.

However, if you have a marketing budget and you want to get your book advertised, you can create an Amazon advertisement. I don't necessarily recommend this unless you are good with the risk of losing money by doing it.

If you really want your book to shine on Amazon, and you don't think it's getting the organic traffic that it should be getting, then, by all means, create an Amazon ad. You can get a targeted Facebook ad created for your book too.

If you feel like you're enough of a tech-savvy marketer to create a Facebook ad on your own, freelance websites, such as Fivver and Upwork, will have folks that can do that for you.

These types of digital ads are great because you can set a firm budget for it. Once that budget has been exhausted, the ad will shut down and stop spending money.

While a paid advertisement is a great way to get your book out there with some money, I always recommend going the route of talking to as many people as you can face-to-face to spread the word. Networking with as many people as you can and giving away your book for free is a safe bet for getting it read.

When you give away a free book, you are simply emailing folks the PDF. This way, you don't have to buy extra copies of it and spend more of your budget.

Of course, there are certain people you might want to give a print copy of your book to for free. You can sign it. There's nothing that feels better than signing your own book! It is a great feeling, so make sure to give out signed copies to some people in your network.

If you're set on having your next book come from a traditional publisher, then give signed copies of your book to people that might have an opportunity to get you in touch with a traditional publisher. This could ultimately increase your visibility as an author one day.

Moving copies of your book and getting it read, takes boots on the ground. It involves talking to people and being bold.

Start with Amazon and Facebook advertisements first if you want to go the paid ad route. From my experience, I don't think Google pay-per-click ads work very well for selling a book. I don't recommend LinkedIn ads either. I also certainly never encourage using Twitter ads, because Twitter ads are traditionally a lot less impactful than Facebook ads (and less targeted to the specific audience that you want to reach).

These are just my opinions, though, and things can always change. These social media and technology companies often make drastic updates and changes to their services at any point, so whatever ends up working for you—more power to you. Sometimes marketing can be very unpredictable, and when you find success from an unlikely source, stick with it! Take the wins wherever you can get them.

There is a lot of "trial and error" involved in marketing.

People might be targeting you to make an appearance at a book fair. I have received calls from strangers (that probably bought my contact information) asking me to appear at random book fairs throughout the United States. They want me to pay hundreds of dollars for this. I kindly decline every time. They are persistent, and each time I politely decline.

You have to be very careful about this. There are companies out there that create (what are essentially) sham book fairs, and they only do it to increase their revenue by getting authors to pay exorbitant fees to enter their book fairs.

I do not recommend joining a book fair where you have to pay a high fee to get in. In general, that money will go way further if you spend it on Facebook or Amazon ads.

That's just my opinion, and again, feel free to research whatever you think is going to give your budget the best bang for its buck.

Don't stop being hungry about gaining your book exposure! As long as you stay polite and friendly, there are many different ways to explore doing it for free, and consistency is the key.

Your book doesn't have to have its own website, but it does need you to be its number one salesperson. It needs you to be the driving force behind its outreach. Talking to people and utilizing the "word of mouth" marketing tactic is a long, continuous journey.

You should be stacking up Amazon reviews if you want your book to sell. The more Amazon reviews you have, the more people will ultimately see your book.

CHAPTER 8

How Lifestyle Impacts Your Publishing Goals

Your lifestyle will impact your writing style. This means you have to be honest with yourself about what is a reasonable writing goal, given your life's responsibilities and free time.

You also have to understand things like what time of day tends to be your most productive time for writing. Are you a morning writer? Or does your brain fire off more synapses in the evening? If possible, write when you tend to be most productive.

It is hard to balance out every other priority in your life and write a book. You have to stay focused and understand that when it's time to write, it's time to write. You can't always afford to wait until your brain feels "inspired" to write.

I find it really hard to write an entire chunk of my book in one sitting. This is known as binge writing.

Most people will struggle with trying to be a binge writer. Typically speaking, it is simply not a sustainable habit.

For someone who has a full-time job and kids, it can be very difficult to find the time to write a book. I think it is important that you build sustainable writing habits and remain honest with yourself about how long it will take you to write a book.

It's ok if it takes you a decade. This is not a competition, and it is certainly not a sprint! As long as you are consistently making an effort towards reaching your goal. Do not put the manuscript away for long stretches of time.

Some folks create artificial deadlines for their writing goals, so they will stick to building a sustainable writing habit.

For example, they claim they will write Chapter 1 in the next month, and then for Chapter 2, they will give themselves three months, etc. This is fine, but creating artificial deadlines can be tough because there are no stakes or consequences for missing the deadline.

If you miss a deadline at your job, the consequence may be that you will be fired! This keeps you focused since the deadlines have real stakes in the real world. With that in mind, it's tough to stick to artificial deadlines for some folks. If there is a way to create meaningful stakes for yourself, then go for it! Maybe you can bet your friend a pricey dinner at a nice restaurant that you will write the first four chapters in four months.

When you set deadlines for yourself, you want to be realistic about what is possible given your current lifestyle. The last thing you want to do is set unreasonable expectations and create burnout. Burnout could lead to someone giving up on writing altogether.

When I write, I set an exact amount of time to write each day and stick to it. I find that if I write too much in one day, the quality begins to dip. I might start to write things that simply don't make sense! I'm honest with myself, and I know that it's what will happen if I try to push myself too hard on a given day. With that in mind, I make sure I'm only devoting a maximum of two hours per day to writing.

Maybe your maximum will be longer than that, or maybe it will be shorter. Be aware of what your lifestyle will allow, and whether or not the quality of your writing tends to dip if you write for too long.

I find it very difficult and darn near impossible, to sit down for eight straight hours to write.

This doesn't mean it will be the same for you. Everyone has a different writing style, and creative inspiration strikes people in different ways.

So if you find yourself writing for eight straight hours, entering a flow-like state of psychology, then I think it's important to "make hay while the sun is shining." Keep writing.

If the inspiration is there, and everything is clicking, then, by all means, continue to write until that inspiration leaves. You just never know when those creative juices will come back!

Discovering the writing habit that will work best for you depends on your lifestyle.

When I come home from work, I need some decompression time before I can start writing.

I set a timer on my smartphone, and I know that once that alarm goes off, my decompression time is officially over, and it's time to begin writing.

Again, this was something that was built over time, and it took a while to build this particular habit.

Once I found my groove, it allowed me to write daily around the same time, like clockwork. Once you build writing into your routine, it starts to feel natural. Consistency is the key; the more you do it, the more natural it will feel over time.

I still think that devoting time each day to writing, and making these sacrifices of your time is worth it. Writing a book can be part of your legacy. This can be what you pass on to future generations in your family. They'll get a chance to learn about you through the written word.

How beautiful is that?

Let's be clear, no matter what your life situation is; you do, in fact, have time to write a book. It doesn't matter if you're retired, and it doesn't matter if you have a full-time job with screaming children running around. It's a matter of discipline, proper communication with your spouse/partner (should you have one), and being honest with yourself as to how bad you really want to write this book.

The good news is that the actual opportunity to self-publish a book has never been easier. The bad news is that our lives seem like they are busier than ever these days. This is why it's crucial to have the discipline to avoid watching two hours of Disney+ or Netflix at night when you could either be writing your book or putting forth research for your book.

I want to emphasize that research for your book might be as important as the actual writing.

The act of "writing your book" doesn't always have to be putting pen to paper. As long as you're doing something to move your book forward, that can be considered writing. It's important to broaden your definition of "writing." If you've designated 5 p.m. to 6 p.m. every day towards writing your book, some days you may not feel inspired to write. On those days, it's important to learn things about KDP's self-publishing platform or conduct other research that will move the production of your book forward.

It's important to do research about how you'll price your book too. Anything you can do that helps move the success of self-publishing your book forward during those designated "writing times" is crucially important.

This is how you build the proper habits that you'll need to complete this project.

Writing a book is a lofty goal, yet highly achievable, given what's possible in today's digital environment.

There's a reason why people find it to be such an incredible life achievement to write a book. It takes a lot of discipline, effort, and consistency. These are skills not everyone has the ability to combine, given the time and energy needed to produce a decent book.

Many people have the idea to write a book, yet don't have the discipline to execute it.

You may be suspect of your skills as a writer, but I think it's important to note that there's a lot of help available to edit and produce the contents of your book.

However, be careful if you have hired a freelancer for editorial assistance if they are doing too much of your ghostwriting.

You don't want these individuals to help *too* much because this book is *your* legacy and should be written in *your* original voice, but they can help a writer who may be "stuck."

It is helpful to lean on the support of editors and ghostwriters, but make sure this book reflects your original thought processes. This book is something that future generations will identify you with, so do it in your voice as much as is possible.

I always encourage you to utilize an editor, no matter how gifted a writer you are.

This is because there may be something you don't notice that an editor will find. On the other hand, hiring a ghostwriter (someone to write the actual copy of your book) can be a slippery slope.

Freelance labor is great for hiring someone to copy-edit your manuscript when you have the first draft completed (so they can find grammatical errors, etc.) and to assist you with some of the technical aspects of self-publishing. You don't have to be tech-savvy to publish a book, but there are things that may take you a lot longer to do within the KDP self-publishing platform that a freelancer might be able to help with.

This includes formatting your book before you submit the manuscript to KDP. Formatting your manuscript so it can be published as a book with KDP is something many people can do, so it's relatively inexpensive to hire someone to do it for you.

I want you to utilize your designated writing time towards doing anything and everything that helps move your book forward. Even if that means using designated writing time to learn how to use websites to hire freelance talent. This is something productive that's helping you reach your ultimate goal of self-publishing a book.

Expanding your definition of writing can help you on days you don't feel very inspired to write.

We're not robots. We are all human. There will be days where you just don't feel like your Hemingway genes are flowing. On those days, use that designated "writing time" to conduct research. It doesn't matter how menial the research may seem, as long as it helps move the production of your book forward, it counts!

There is a reason you're reading this book right now. You have a story that you want to tell the world. You have a legacy you want to leave. No matter what age you are, your book will be around forever.

To get the book done, you should be serious about carving out consistent, designated writing time within your lifestyle, no matter how hectic it may be. It starts with being aware of what time in your schedule you can realistically spend towards creating this book. Maybe writing every day is just not possible given your lifestyle, but that is ok. Maybe it's every other day, you can afford, or maybe it's just twice a week.

Be honest with yourself and know what your particular lifestyle will allow, but then be consistent!

Even if it is literally one hour a week that you can devote towards writing. If that is all you can spare, you cannot be upset. It may take you 15 years to write this book, but if that's realistically all the time that you have to devote to it, then so be it!

As long as you are relentlessly consistent with devoting that one hour a week to doing everything you can to write this book, then you're doing everything within your power to achieve this goal.

You should be happy with yourself as long as you were completely honest when you looked at your lifestyle, and you saw that there was realistically only one hour a week you could devote towards writing this book. If you did everything within your control to create this book during that hour, then that is all you can do.

I think it's silly to get upset about things that are out of our control. (Of course, it's not easy, but neither is writing a book!)

Look at your other life priorities and assess how important writing this book is to you. Then find the time that's reasonable to be writing each day (or week) and stick to it.

As long as you are driven to have the book published, and you commit to it, you will achieve that goal with dedication and consistency.

CHAPTER 9

Business, Taxes, and Housekeeping Notes

Now that you are about to write and publish your own book, you need to start looking at yourself as an entrepreneur.

As an author, you're creating a product for the world, and in your attempt to do that, you should be viewing yourself as behaving like an entrepreneur/businessperson. This means tracking your expenses!

I know it can be difficult or seem intimidating for those without a business background. A business may not interest you nor come naturally for you, but it is very important.

As an aspiring writer in college, I was very averse to the business side of things. I wanted to have nothing to do with it. I just wanted to write. I was convinced writing was my only calling. I studied print journalism and figured the rest would work itself out.

The truth is life is more complicated than that.

If you want to write as a full-time job, then more than ever, you have to look at yourself as a business. Freelance writing gigs are the norm; salaries are increasingly harder to come by. Gone are the days of a comfortable salary that awaits a newspaper writer after paying their dues for a couple of decades.

Getting a little experience in bookkeeping and handling the business side of things is no longer a skill that's "nice to have" as a writer, it's a must.

One of the major tasks within the process of becoming a published author is making sure you track your expenses and (eventually) revenues.

You have to account for all of these numbers. Royalties you earn on books must be reported to your state and federal governments as part of your tax obligations.

When you start creating revenue from your book sales, by law, you will need to be reporting that income so you can be taxed accordingly. Failing to track your expenses is an easy mistake to make for a first-time author.

You must be diligent about tracking your expenses. Expenses are what it costs you to write books. You are entitled to write-off the expenses you incur while writing, publishing, and marketing your book.

This means that any freelance help or services you paid for to create your book should be accounted for carefully. Save those receipts! (By the way, most receipts these days are digital, so print them off and have a hard copy available at all times.)

I make sure I write off all the proper business expenses as necessary, but I'm not a CPA, and sometimes it can be confusing, so I consult my tax accountant. As long as you are not doing anything with your income that is incredibly elaborate, a standard tax consultant with H&R Block should be able to help you.

If your book starts to bring in large revenues, you may have to start paying your taxes quarterly or monthly (as opposed to waiting until the end of the year when you file your tax return).

As the more money gets involved, the more important it is that you get in contact with an accountant (or someone who's certified to do tax returns) and ask them about this.

The United States government doesn't like it when you wait until the end of the year to pay all of your taxes if you're making a lot of money from book sales. They want to get that money faster, and if you aren't paying the proper threshold on a regular basis (quarterly, monthly), you may run into a tax penalty.

A qualified tax professional will be able to help you sort this all out. You just have to make sure you play by the rules, and since you will be paying your fair share of taxes on your book's revenues, you owe it to yourself to be equally as disciplined with tracking your expenses.

You need to start looking at yourself as someone who is now professionally engaging within a business endeavor, and you are taking on the financial risks to create this book. The moment you start receiving royalties on this book, you are no longer a hobbyist. Your tax obligations require you to be a disciplined bookkeeper.

There are different ways to set up your business account. You can certainly start an LLC or something of that nature (S-Corp and C-Corp).

Consider discussing this with a small business expert in your area. Most communities in the United States have access to the Society of Retired Business Executives (SCORE). These volunteers coach people about their small business enterprises. Therefore, I would recommend being in contact with a SCORE representative who will provide information about what to do as your writing turns into a business endeavor.

Probably the easiest and least expensive way to start creating your own business entity as a self-publisher is to become a sole proprietor. I would probably recommend you start as a sole proprietor before venturing into more complicated infrastructures such as LLC or S-Corp. This is a general statement, though, and whatever works best for you should supersede my advice.

The major downfall to being a sole proprietor comes up if a lawsuit rears its ugly head. If you are sued due to something you've done professionally (i.e., libel), which is obviously very possible in this time that we live in, you will not be able to protect your personal assets—because as a sole proprietor your personal assets are looked at as the same as your business assets.

This means if you get sued as a sole proprietor, your personal assets will be potentially vulnerable in the lawsuit. This means you could end up losing your personal possessions.

Scary stuff. Just be careful, though, and understand there are legal risks associated with self-publishing.

You do expose yourself to some extra risk there, but again, if you're just writing a book and doing your due diligence to avoid plagiarism and libel, then you should be fine. I would not worry about being sued.

If you plan to continuously pump out books and you plan to devote your life to being a self-published author, then maybe you should look at creating a more sophisticated business structure than a sole proprietorship.

To figure this out (at essentially no cost or risk), you should talk to a volunteer with SCORE. This is probably your best bet because these friendly folks offer their services for free. You can email them or get in contact with them for a phone call if you have questions about the business aspect of self-publishing.

No matter what business entity you choose, track all of your expenses and royalties. Those numbers must be accounted for when you pay taxes.

The point is you need to start looking at what you're doing as a serious professional endeavor now. Don't wait until your local and federal governments start paying attention because you owe them extra taxes.

If you end up losing money by, say, engaging in advertising or hiring an editor, then you want to make sure that it's being reflected in your tax returns.

What's fair is fair here, folks, if you take risks to sell your books (i.e., paid advertising) and it flops, then you shouldn't be taxed on that advertising campaign at the end of the year. This becomes something crucially important should you engage with paid marketing campaigns to promote your work.

You don't need pricey accounting software unless you are planning to launch a serious business enterprise with lots of cash flowing through your business.

Most folks can get by with a spreadsheet, but consult your tax professional and/or local SCORE volunteer before you jump into it.

If you're not tech-savvy, and you don't like using things like TurboTax and other tax preparation software, then I'll give a plug to the good old H&R Block. They seem to be around a lot.

H&R Block can be expensive if you really crunch the numbers, but again, it might be worth it since you can come into a friendly office and speak with someone about properly filing taxes related to your book.

You can give them an idea of the number of expenses and revenues (albeit this is hard to predict) that may be involved, and it could save you many headaches.

If you're not tech-savvy, then try to utilize the brick and mortar tax preparation services. I just enjoy going into an office and talking things out more than having to use tax preparation software. Talking to someone in person about my taxes puts a human touch on things.

If you have a question pop up, they answer it right then and there. It's more enjoyable than dealing with "chatbots" for my customer service needs. I consider myself a pretty tech-savvy guy, but I prefer to talk to the people face to face who are preparing my taxes.

I don't know if I'll use them forever, but H&R Block here in the United States has gotten the job done for me and has helped me set up quarterly tax payments (for both state and federal obligations).

I'm definitely making sure I account for all my expenses and revenues. That was something that became really important to me when I started to write books on my own.

I knew that I was spending money and taking on risk to have this book created and marketed. I was spending money on things like Facebook and Google ads. With that in mind, I definitely wanted to make sure I was tracking those expenses because that's only fair.

The bottom line is if you're going to be taxed on your revenue, then you definitely need to be accounting for all the expenses that it costs you to create this book.

As a writer, I know that the business side of things is not glamorous. It's not the first thing you think of when you want to create your dream book, but it's definitely something you have to account for and cannot ignore.

CHAPTER 10

Final Thoughts and Pep Talk

After I wrote my first book, I was pleasantly surprised by how many people came from seemingly out of nowhere to congratulate me. It was one of the most overwhelming and humbling occurrences of my life.

A lot of people I never expected to be supportive (frankly, I thought maybe they forgot about me) reached out to congratulate me after I posted about it on social media.

Most of these people (if not all of them) went on to purchase the book. These are people who I hadn't spoken with in years; they were fascinated that I had completed an entire book. They peppered me with questions about how I did it and found the time.

The whole situation of people delivering me kind words and purchasing the book, even when I didn't really ask them to buy it, was humbling. I said I would give them a free PDF of it, but they insisted on purchasing it on Amazon.

Some acquaintances in my life heard about my book through word of mouth, and found it on their own and purchased it.

I was overwhelmed by this support. I always knew that I was a writer and that my love of the written word would cumulate into a book one day. I was humbled by the overwhelmingly positive response to my book. Honestly, people that I never even thought would care were completely and utterly happy for me. The positive vibes created some of the more unexpected and surprisingly pleasant turns of events in my life.

To this day, I am still humbled by all that support that came my way after my first book. All the hard work and time that went into creating it was worth it. That's why I want to encourage you to keep going even when things seem impossible. If you run into a hurdle, find a way to get through it. If you don't feel inspired to write one day, think about how gratifying it will be when you get through this and publish the book.

Nothing topped the joy that came when strangers started emailing me with kind words about my book.

This was because I included a way for people to reach out to me at the end of the book. I wanted folks to have a way to contact me directly with their feedback.

It opened my horizons to new people and brought with it an influx of positive energy.

People say that creating your book is one of the hardest things to do. I've heard folks say that it's akin to one of the toughest "bucket list items" that you could ever create for yourself. I know it's a challenge, but it's far from as difficult as other people tend to make it seem.

I am here to tell you that on the other end of it, there's something beautiful and magical that makes you feel like it was all worth it. It will hit you too if you are resilient and you don't have any quit inside of you.

You really have to change your mindset to make this a reality. You have to know this is not your hobby; creating this book is (at the very least) a part-time job. The dollars and cents that it takes to create this book are no joke. Neither is the royalties that may come later. Those are not hobbyist numbers, and they should be accounted for carefully. You are a professional.

No matter what age you are, this book will live on forever. Be proud and happy after you achieve your goal, but do not expect it to change your life monetarily.

Book sales and future royalties can be very difficult to predict. It's hard to tell which books are going to be the next bestseller. It's like trying to predict which content will go viral on the internet. You really cannot plan it. Viral just seems to happen.

For a first time author, it is possible your book will "go viral," but it's not exactly likely. If your book doesn't sell, do not be discouraged. Remember, you were smart enough to keep your overhead low when creating the book. You did this by using the proper websites to hire freelance labor (Fiverr.com and Upwork.com). You aren't going to have to "break the bank" when getting your book edited and cover created. There are places where you can get the most competitive rates within the freelance talent labor market.

Since you use those tools, you keep your overhead low. There's no need to ever spend more than a couple hundred dollars to create your own book by using freelance talent. In this environment of self-publishing, it's never been cheaper to create your book. Let me remind you that with KDP, you also don't have to buy excessive inventory of your book.

KDP publishes your book on demand. You don't have to put yourself in financial ruins to write a book these days. That's why you don't need to become discouraged if your book doesn't sell.

I did not have expectations for my first book outside of just wanting to make it a reality. When the people came out of nowhere to congratulate me, it changed my life in terms of making me happier. Yes, the book did create some royalties, so it was something I had to track for tax purposes, but it wasn't difficult to stay on top of that. It wasn't life-changing money, but it offset the cost of creating the book and advertising. It was enough to pay for extra copies of my book to give away to friends!

Remember that technology does not have a mind of its own; it treats us all the same. It can be finicky and fickle, like a game of golf, though. Sometimes, systems have bad days. I suppose information technology systems are just like people in that respect. Be patient, resilient, and never be afraid to restart your systems and computers.

Hang in there, folks, technology will eventually become a wonderful tool for you as an author!

After my first book was complete, the next two went a lot smoother.

I did well with the freelance artists I hired on Fiverr.com to design my book's cover and edit my copy. They did great work and were affordable. This made it a no-brainer to select the same talent for my next two books. This saved me a lot of time vetting potential freelance candidates.

It will always take a lot of work to write a book, but the process will get smoother for you if you ever plan on writing a second or third one.

It may take you more time to self-publish a book because self-publishing tools are technology-based, and you have to learn to use them. Remember, though; it's the creative side that's inside of you that matters. Other people may learn how to use technology faster than you, but they may never have the creativity you bring to the table. The real talent to uncover and bring to light is creativity. The technology is just a tool to make your book available for others to consume in mass.

Talent rises to the top in this digital era, because the internet is very democratized. It's a meritocracy as its core.

This means people who are the most creative will eventually rise to the top and be seen. It's not going to be the people that know how to use the technology the best. With this era of technology, those who stand out are the writers that have the actual talent. Publishing your book will be worth it; you might just have to prove how bad you want it, though.

As long as you believe in yourself as a writer/storyteller and you prove that you want it bad enough, believe me, all the hard work will be worth it.

This is probably a labor of love, or a passion project, for you, but down the line when you least expect it, someone will discover your book. This could lead to you selling more copies than you could ever dream.

Future generations of your family will reap the benefits, and a part of your legacy will always be there within this book. There are so many reasons to fight through the hurdles that come your way when you want to self-publish a book. I encourage you to continue that mission through the hardest of times, no matter what obstacles you encounter.

I am always surprised when people review my book, and they say something like, "He has a very nice conversational tone when he writes."

I am thankful for the kind words, but it seems so obvious that this is the only way to write. What other tones could I possibly write in? You have to be yourself. Being yourself is the only thing that separates us from every other oversaturated project or idea on the internet (including a book for sale).

Writing styles that are natural are going to resonate with people because that is the essence of creativity. Your own individuality shines when you write as if you are talking and being yourself. That's really important when it comes to staying original.

If you're writing about a subject you care deeply about, and you sound like yourself, you're knocking off two of the most important checkboxes in writing. Think about it. It is a complete "win-win" if you are writing about something you care about in your own individual voice.

There's nothing more natural (and potentially powerful) than that.

If you have picked a subject you care deeply about, and you continuously sound like yourself when you're writing about it, there is nothing that can stop you.

Don't try to razzle-dazzle your audience with big words (and words that you would never use in normal conversation) when you write. The smartest person and best writer, in my opinion, will only care about making sure the readers understand what they're writing about. Attempting to impress people by the use of "big words" is pointless, in my view.

Nobody likes to pause what they are doing in the middle of reading a book to go consult the dictionary and start looking up the word. The writer decided to use an extremely valuable Scrabble word, and now you're away from the book, looking it up. What a mess.

The author could have done us all a favor and used a more basic word that most people understand. Save me time! I don't want to have to open my smartphone and search on Google for what a word means; there are too many potential distractions when I do that!

Next thing you know, I get a notification in my email app, and I'm distracted for the next two hours. (Admittedly, this is my own fault, but still, I don't want to have to leave what I'm doing when I read to look up a fancy word.)

It happens a lot; people try to use impressive words, but it really just ends up distracting your reader.

I know that sometimes using a fancy word is unavoidable, but I guarantee you it's more avoidable than some writers realize!

As a writer, you're going to reach your audience better and more effectively by using simple and plain language and doing so in your own voice.

Always consider your readers and make things easiest for them. If you know your entire audience is going to have college and graduate degrees, then yes, you can use a couple of more high caliber words that maybe explain something a little better than a simpler word. But again, why not make your book open to the most people possible? You can do that by using plain and simple language.

I'm a lucky enough person to have spent the majority of my career writing and communicating as a professional.

I enjoy communicating with people more than just about anything. This made writing my first book an easy decision. I always thought I would do it, but until I actually sat down and took the time to learn how to do it and build a writing habit, it was never going to be a reality.

If you carve out that time to write, you'll be amazed by what will happen when you're consistent. The book will become a reality. Publishing your own book can be a unique and magical experience.

I wish you the best with this deeply fulfilling endeavor. Happy self-publishing, my friends, and please try like heck to enjoy your time doing it.

Moreover, and most important of all, never give up.

REFERENCES

Bolt, Chandler. Published.: The Proven Path From Blank Page to Published Author. 2016.

Flynn, Pat. (2019, July). The Smart Passive Income (SPI) podcast: Episode 381, Self-Publishing versus Traditional Publishing

Skarupski, Kimberly A. WAG Your Work: Writing Accountability Groups: Bootcamp for Increasing Scholarly Productivity. 2018.

Vonnegut, Kurt. (1980, June) How to write with style. Institute of Electrical and Electronics Engineers' journal, Transactions on Professional Communications.

ABOUT THE AUTHOR

Casey Callanan is the owner of Clear Contender Media. A company he started to further his life goals of helping the world communicate better. Casey is a graduate of West Virginia University's Reed School of Media and holds a Master of Business Administration (MBA) from Louisiana State University Shreveport's College of Business, Education, and Human Development.

He is a lifelong writer and boxing enthusiast; he believes the same principles that make a great prizefighter (perseverance, resilience, and the will to be great) translate rather perfectly to the world of communications.

As a successful podcast host with a background in journalism, communications, and digital marketing, he's in the business of helping people communicate better one story at a time.

His other books include:

- **How to Podcast When You Aren't Tech Savvy:** *A Clear-Cut Book about How (and Why) to Launch a Podcast*
- **Altmetrics for Academic Faculty:** *A Comprehensive Guide to Getting Tactical with the Tools of Altmetrics*
- **Anxiety Relief from Online Bullies:** Guidance to Fight Negative Vibes and Internet Trolls

THANK YOU

I appreciate you taking the time to read this book. I'd love to hear from you. Feel free to leave a helpful review on Amazon, or find my contact information on **ClearContender.com** and drop me a line!

I wish you all the best and send you my sincerest gratitude.

With warmest regards,

Casey Callanan

Learn more at **ClearContender.com**

www.ingramcontent.com/pod-product-compliance
Lightning Source LLC
Chambersburg PA
CBHW020534160726
47992CB00005BA/2381